CLACKAMAS LITERARY REVIEW

2014
Volume XVIII

Clackamas Community College
Oregon City, Oregon

CLACKAMAS LITERARY REVIEW

Editor in Chief

Ryan Davis

Associate Editors

Trevor Dodge

Matthew Warren

Assistant Editors

Andrew Accuardi   Memorie Brown   Tyler Harper

Emily Horger   Matthew Morrissey   Dylan Plotner

Morgaine Stamme

Cover Art

Charles Reneau

"Rock in Stream"

Journal Design

Matthew Warren

Clackamas Literary Review
19600 Molalla Avenue, Oregon City, Oregon 97045
ISBN: 978-0-9796882-6-3
Printed by Lightning Source
www.clackamasliteraryreview.org

CONTENTS

Editor in Chief's Note

We are all of a place. We are all a place ourselves. The words in these pages carry us home, away, and back. A specific point on the map emerges when Sandra Rokoff-Lizut begins her poem with the words,

Low-lying
ribbons of fog
circle the mountain
settle at its base
freeing treetops.

I have seen this on many mornings—this is my mountain. Yet, it is yours too.

Matt Schumacher paints a triptych of a poem, moving us through the Pacific Northwest, from Lolo Pass to Zigzag Mountain to Lost Lake, each location unique, though similar, if only we would notice.

We ask, *Am I there? Or am I here?*

We realize, *I am in both places. Those places are me.*

As we move through the forest, we are reminded by Schumacher to "Slow down. Please." This is the best advice.

Welcome home,
Ryan Davis
Editor in Chief

Lending a Book

Richard Luftig

is like saying goodbye
to your college sweetheart
who is leaving to study in France;
she swears to come back to you
but even if she does it might

be years later when she is worn
and worse for wear, her spine
in disrepair, her jacket reeking
of cigarette smoke. Or perhaps
you are like that fisherman

alone at sea, always disappointed,
yet willing to cast your net
upon the cold-cod waters,
but knowing all the while
that it always turns up empty.

But still you'll do it, recalling
how it is better to give, to share,
not keeping your gifts hidden under
some bushel basket or sowing seeds
without worrying about the returns.

Heart Mark Where the Sky Was

Christopher T. Keaveney

9/11/2011, Edgewater, New Jersey

The way clouds pucker
around the wound.
I was there,
so were you
when summer seemed to lose
its bearing
and the ice on the saucer
slid in impossible angles of abandon.

That sound you can barely make out
from this distance
is the sound of practiced hands
shielding the ears of the uninitiated
from a song hung
on bones of glass.
It was not supposed to be this way,
but the winds that hug the ground
remain jaundiced and skittering.

That light you can almost discern with the naked eye
is a curio bouncing in the mirror
clutched by a baby
in the back of a plane barreling
toward anxious grandparents,
a hologram in the bluest sky
in the memory of a man
with one hand raised
pointing,
the other covering his mouth.

Campobello Island

Kathleen M. McCann

for Carla

There you are leaning against the boat's hull
in a framed pose of happiness.
Your smile belies the wood's pinch,
an urge to straighten up and fix
the headband losing to long hair,
reach for the backpack's cigarettes.
Twenty years and still you smoke.

Kind or unkind, the years
return to one another.
And we the same,
for the good times: lusty laughter,
a cove pretty enough
to break you,
if the water did not.

The Six-Legged Solution

Sean Gill

We had a roach problem. And when I say we had a roach problem, I mean we *really* had a roach problem.

My older sister had lived there for over a year before I moved in— "there" being a modest two-bedroom apartment in upper Greenpoint, a neighborhood that had remained essentially Polish despite the northward tiptoeing of trust-funded gentrification. I'd always theorized that Greenpoint was so fiercely Polish that it would be the last of the major Brooklyn neighborhoods to lose its old-world flavor entirely.

I first arrived at 3:00 A.M. on a Monday in June, and as I approached the threshold of my new home (clutching some plastic storage unit holdover from my dorm life) I was greeted with the splashing of a startling, cool liquid on my face. I froze instinctively and took a step back. Up on the fifth floor, an old man in a discolored wifebeater was pouring out a plastic bottle of unknown origin. I stared up, and he stared back. The exchange must have only lasted three or four seconds, but it felt like an eternity. Just when I expected him to shout down an apology, he tilted his bottle to begin pouring anew, and I stepped inside the door to avoid the foul cascade. What a christening!

We lived in a slum, but the rent was expensive. Neither my sister nor I had steady employment, so we lived our lives like drowning souls, our watery flailings being the odd jobs and the temp jobs, the cater-waiting and the like. We had an entire Rolodex of temp agencies and employment companies who would occasionally call us up, offering shifts. We shared a cell phone (which naturally presented a whole host of logistical difficulties), and whenever it would ring, I became filled with a terrible sensation of obligation and dread. Soon, the little electronic song that played when the phone rang enacted a Pavlovian response of nausea and distress. Though I changed the ringer, soon the new song was filling me with revulsion, even when it was my friends who would call.

The human mind can get used to anything. It keeps us sane, I suppose, but sometimes it can deceive us; it can prevent us from realizing that we're swirling around at the bottom of the toilet bowl.

It started small, as it often does. It's New York City. You *will* see roaches—you simply kill them and move on with your life. However, we began seeing an irregular amount of roaches, of all varieties. Tiny ones, wispy medium-sized "German" ones, and the massive creatures colloquially referred to as "water bugs." Our landlady Moira had ceased her monthly roach spraying; a cost-cutting measure of some kind, I imagine. We couldn't afford an exterminator, and the roaches laughed at our traps, purchased at the 99-cent store down the block. I bought the bug bomb for $5.99, but there were plenty of warnings on about explosions and turning off gas mains, and in the midst of a near-constant scent of natural gas it suddenly seemed too great a risk. Therefore, we stuck to the tried and true "smash 'em when ya see 'em" method.

We waged war. Sometimes at night, I'd walk into the kitchen, flip on the lights, and start smashing. At first, I'd see three or four. I'd get them all. After a few months, I was seeing what had to be *hundreds* of them, swarming on the floor and on the counters. I might smash as many as forty—and that's no exaggeration—before they escaped to their nooks and crannies and wall fissures. Each time we opened the silverware drawer, there'd be a whole gang of them in there, too. It was revolting. I'd kill all the roaches in the drawer, fully rewash the silverware, and then replace it. As time went on, I'd only rinse the silverware. By the end of our time there, I didn't even care if my forks bore the impression of cockroach feet—I'd use them anyway.

They took the oven one summer day. They never gave it back. I was about to roast some frozen fish when I made my discovery. The fish was in my hand, thawed, pan-seasoned, and at the ready. Upon opening the oven I was greeted with a profusion of roaches, the awful things crawling and wriggling and ejecting egg cases out of their behinds. We never used the oven again. During the occasional midnight smashing, after the majority had vanished into the walls, I'd open up the oven and smash a few, but generally their presence there was so upsetting, I'd quickly shut the door. They made it into the fridge, too, but I suppose it wasn't a very practical habitat for them, so they never really took hold there in a big way.

One morning I had a temp job at ten, and my sister had one at eight. I heard the door slam as she left the apartment, but then it opened as she returned, almost immediately. She came into my room, and I stirred.

"Holy shit, the biggest water bug I have ever seen is out there in the hallway!"

"Good," I said. "Why don't you smash it?"

"I'm in a hurry, dude. I just wanted to tell you, so that you don't let it in when you leave."

"Thank you," I murmured, drifting off. Predictably, two hours later, it was waiting for me in the bathroom, almost as if it knew I'd be urinating, barefoot, when it decided to show itself. The behemoth entered my line of vision, very slowly. It approached my foot. It lumbered. It was big enough to *lumber*. I've never seen a roach that big, before or since (and that's even counting the African hissing variety that I don't think ought to count because they merely look like big dumb beetles—they lack that hairy-legged, feathery, filthy quality). I stepped out of the room, looking for the first object I could lay my hands on that would be capable of slaying the brute. My hand grasped a dustpan and as I brought it down on the thing with a squash, the roach *screamed*. God help me, it *screamed*. It was a shrill, bubbling squawk, like a sound a chicken or a dog's chew toy might make. I hammered it again with the dustpan and took another look. It was lying there in its own brown and yellow guts, legs swimming in the air, helplessly. I hammered it again. Still it twitched. I hit it again and again and again. I hit it twelve times before it finally became still and died. I was peculiarly drained for the rest of the day. I think it was the largest creature I had ever killed, and it felt substantial. (I don't think we can call it a bug anymore—it was an *animal*.) I felt the same way a few months later when I had to hammer a rat to death with a plastic mop handle, and a few months after that when I used a brick to euthanize a trapped mouse who had somehow kept on ticking despite a bifurcated spine. I wondered if having to engage in these everyday brutalities was slowly forging me into a different person.

I remember very distinctly the first time a roach touched me when I was naked. I was drying off in my room after a shower, and a bold little bastard began clambering up my leg. I brushed him away and smashed him with my slipper, but afterward I was in a state of agitation. My nakedness was vulnerability and that roach had seized his moment. There was a degree of fearfulness and insecurity from this point forward. I was often convinced that something was crawling on me; I'd feel the twinge of an arm hair and be sure of it. Most of the time I was wrong, but you only have to be right one time out of a hundred to keep fanning those paranoid flames. They knew how to really get to me then, and perhaps the ultimate indignity came soon afterward.

As far as rooms went, the bathroom was one of the safer ones. I killed only maybe ten or so a day in there. It didn't make sense, because it boasted even more water-bearing pipes than the kitchen, and water is a cockroach's preferred form of nourishment. Nevertheless, I often let my guard down while I was in the bathroom.

I used to like taking long Saturday morning showers after a particularly arduous work week (and the shenanigans of the Friday night before). It was a warm, soothing rebirth, focusing my creative energies for the following two days that I could dedicate to my art. Of course, this wasn't entirely successful on the weekends when I had a cater-waitering gig, but for the most part, I kept my weekends free.

Regardless, as I began this particular Saturday morning shower, my mind was abuzz with ideas for a new short film. As I lathered up my dollar-store loofah, I was thinking about alternate dimensions through holes in the wall and other mystical methods of escape from a world gone sour. A few minutes of hearty scrubbing had passed before I noticed that several of the hateful things had died inside my sponge the night before, and that I was depositing roach parts and soap lather across my naked body. According to my sister, at this point there was a shout from the bathroom, but I do not recall making such a noise. There was an initial trauma as my mind tried to make sense of what I was seeing—bits of wing and whiskered leg and antennae were mixed with soapy foam, *everywhere*. At the time I didn't give it much thought, but now I am convinced that the sheer number of body parts indicated that no less than four roaches must have expired inside my loofah. Why would four roaches make the joint decision to crawl into a loofah and die? Perhaps they did it to get to the remnants of water inside, but why would they do that when a leaky faucet not two feet away could have provided them with ample refreshment?

I remember reading a possibly apocryphal story about G. Gordon Liddy eating a rat to overcome his fear of them. Perhaps there *is* something to that—you don't quite feel the same way about roaches once you've bathed yourself in their viscera. I still hated them and I was still repulsed by them to be sure, but now there wasn't really anything *more* that they could do to me. They had thrown at me the worst that they had to offer, and I had survived.

Later, they tried something similar—I stepped into the shower to find that two egg cases had hatched and several hundred baby roaches were swarming about, not sure what to do next in this vast, white porcelain world they had inherited. I rinsed my feet of their corpses and killed every last one of them with balled-up toilet paper. They couldn't get to me anymore.

Above North Carolina

Ricardo Pau-Llosa

How to think the land
is not a wall of peeling paint,
although these farms reveal

the old intention to fructify
by straight-edge. Yet parcels
do not claim all. Fragrant

fragments of torn and green
unscroll what kins parchments,
recalling museum displays

where lyric Greek isles
are ochre-pathed by script
against a glass. Lost utterance

is surmised in leaps
to right the sallow luster.
It is dawn's work, this tension

of forms dappling, reefing scandent
to the horizon's terse. Here and there,
trompe l'oeil above river and lake,

a gathered spill of cloud will neither
dissipate nor abjure the ground,
inventing, rather, fog when all

that's gained is a stranded bloom
of white confusion. Earlier,
at the Greensboro airport,

the sun stirred the minions
who waited at Gate 50
in a drowse of scattered boulders.

Later, settled into journey,
a three-year old boy behind me
will ask his mother why the plane

is not moving. I almost want
to tell Little Jason: I promise you,
nothing, no mercy or mission

of silenced love, will hold us in stillness.
See us there, grey and quick
against pages of clouds, a Braille denied.

Power Song

Mike Pulley

On the back patio of this café
in an old gold mining town
of the Sierra foothills,
I dine alone with my latest volume.
I am entombed in a shivering creek
flowing beneath the boards of my feet,
listening inside the water music,
drinking in shards of light
to shrink my fear of power.

This is a porch song I sing as I sit
reading my book of brains,
the fresh pages so white in the sunlight,
my unheard speech shrinking
as the amorphous space
within my inner world deepens.
The sparkling sunlight on the table
blown by the wind
through the shadows—
the bright excitement within
my private world,
the splashing harmonies—

this is a song about how to get power
into my veins, a prayer
for power, a prayer
for keeping it,
even in this public place
amidst the movement
of the servers
and the sparse chatter,
the peace of light-glow
and liquid hymns
inspirational inside
the depths of my becoming
who I am.

Who am I to be afraid
of the light?

Who am I to sing for
in the dark?

January

After a watercolor by Myrna Pulley

Is it the glow of an arch I see
in this coldest of coldest months—
the glimmer over the hill I turn to
in a time of deep thinking
when the frozen white world
awakens me, chilled in my skin,
to look up expectantly
to the sky's distracting shimmers?
That other white sea in front of me
like an enormous wave
rising on its frozen shoulder,
fractured only by farmhouse, trees—
some green, reaching—others in skeletal
dormancy, the remnants of the road—
two gray snakes with unseen
snake heads behind the crest,
and those resistant rocks like fish statuary
fresh risen from the icy brine,
their durable bodies hot enough to melt
the best that snowflakes have to offer,

sure like that flickering insignia
embedded in the clouds.
My cold eyes look up to it
longing for the other side of winter.
I name it my pet neon chevron
suspended like hope in a pastel horizon.
I call it my darling little lightshow,
my sweet tiny rainbow of worship.

Bored Game

Bray McDonald

Ranting it isn't fair
when what I wanted would not have me.
Trying to avoid despair
with heretical hyperbole.
Imitating the King of Broadway
with a free card at every jail
and railways and hotels
and Park Place still for sale.
Pretending I'm still captain of my fate
and my soul in control
I attempt to appease what I cannot sate.
Puzzled by pieces of the whole
I'm a haberdasher stalking the unknown roads
with other pretenders and hackneyed toads.

Mandamus

Thomas Elson

Maria felt the familiar touch of Wanda's two fingers on her lips. After Wanda retracted her hand, Maria inhaled. No one noticed their cigarette. Smoking was forbidden, pretending was not. They leaned back as if in unison, and surveyed the room. A single curtainless window exposed a residential area with full trees, deep front lawns, aboveground houses, with newer cars and tricycles in driveways.

Judy, the group leader, maneuvered her high-back chair into their group circle. She asked Maria to begin. Maria jerked her chair back. Her legs shot forward. Heads snapped, judgmental mouths stilled, cross-talk, opinions, insightful face-slaps silenced. Maria said, "You, what? You couldn't possibly know how Wanda and I feel. And before you say it, if you tell us you feel our pain, we'll die."

Maria no longer faked compliance within this imposed reality. Refused to establish a permanent residence, chose to visit from time to time. She had created a physical distance from her early days, separated the years, placed them on a shelf. That decision held until the second year of her third marriage.

Before her hospitalization, Maria stood in a doorway at the top of the stairs, as stoic as a Wyeth canvas, and looked at her daughter, Theresa. And regretted an earlier impulse.

That afternoon, with Theresa nestled inside the car after school, Maria said, "Theresa, let's have an adventure; we'll go see something."

"Where? Where to, Mommy?"

"To a house, you'll like it."

The house, two stories with a finished basement, on the market for months, price reduced. Maria entered despite memories. "Mommy, let's go down there." Pointed to the basement, then ran. Maria hurried to keep up, grasped the handrails, balanced her shoulder against the wall.

Heard her daughter's instructions, "Follow me, follow me."

Responded to her daughter bounding downstairs, "Theresa, get back up here."

Theresa heard the command, as many children do, as a suggestion. Maria made a decision, pirouetted. Moments later, after she thanked to realtor, and placed Theresa's hand firmly in hers, Maria hurried to the car, and trembled.

Maria remembered basements not as a family areas, not as laundry rooms, nor storage spaces, she remembered basements as crypts. Hers had been seven-feet high, wide enough for two mattresses on a dirt floor next to four stolen lawn chairs near a green wooden park bench.

As a child, in what Maria called old town, she had hurried to keep up—to get out. Today, Maria equates basements with being pulled, forced.

"Mommy, you acted funny in there."

"That I did." *But never again.* Squeezed the steering wheel, asked, "What do you think about where we live now?"

"I like it."

"How come?"

"I like the elevators."

After dinner in their fourth floor condo with a well-stocked refrigerator and closets, Maria asked Theresa, "What would you like to do for your eighth birthday?"

"To see where you were a little girl. Where you used to live."

Her little girl had become what Maria prayed for—even though Theresa's independent streak had emerged earlier than expected. Maria planned on the streak magically appearing on Teresa's twenty-first birthday, not before her eighth.

One week later, they crossed the Ninnescah River for their three-hour drive to old town.

Maria felt the double thumping of old town's brick streets. She had forgotten the old limestone street posts, dry goods stores, walls with time-faded frescos advertising long-shuttered businesses—the Barron Theater, Briggs Hotel, P-K Pharmacy, Gayle's Ladies Wear. She made a diversion, north past the Rhode Island depot, grain elevators alongside with the other usual settlements historically found on that side of the tracks. Stopped in front of an ancient red brick building. Three classrooms for eight grades next to the rectory beside the church in front of the simulated log cabin meeting hall up the hill from the convent. Maria's coming of age in a half city block of church and school.

They walked toward the school, and Maria felt Theresa's energy; saw a pale black-and-white image of herself as a child watching from the curb across the street. Mothers lifted their children, hugged them. Children did not flinch, but smiled when placed inside cars, handed snacks. Children eating. *Chewing, actually chewing. I don't remember chewing anything after school. Just sitting on that curb and wanting to live someplace safe.* Children edged closer, parents looked down, hugged, smiled again. Warm cars, food, safe evenings together—safe weekends. *Parents doing what they're supposed to. Not doing that other stuff.*

Yesterday's images in black and white—the nuns, the children after school, a young Maria on the curb. Listened as Wanda told her story: In the days before after-school learning centers, Maria walked from her three-room grade school, its red bricks, well-ordered, nun-enforced 1950s discipline, and waited across the street.

As a child, Maria sensed the stares, masks, avoidance, the words a confluence of judgment, summary, and aversion. "Look at her bare legs. She looks like she never eats. Does she wear that dress all week?" Heard as they walked away to their cars, safe homes. Waves of emptiness. Defenseless, gates broken. Sat alone until dark, knew what awaited her: a basement, her father's demands.

Maria's father hauled a duffel bag of abuse and invective marinated in bitterness fueled by what others made him do. Remained in a state of war that required artillery, paranoia, enemies. Maria was one of his enemies.

Her mother was rented-out for long stretches of time, used her body to survive, numbed herself with alcohol. Maria never knew where her mother went; saw her mother only as silent and unsmiling. When in the house, her mother kept Maria's father relaxed. Maria learned early that life grew easier when men were relaxed. After which they slept.

Unable to protect herself, she offered Maria motherly guidance. "Just do what he says." Maria listened to her parents yell, watched her mother pack, and leave Maria alone with him.

Maria leaned her head against hospital the wall as Wanda talked, felt less pressure whenever Wanda talked. "When Maria entered that basement, her eyes adjusted slowly. As a little girl, Maria knew what to expect." As an adult, she could articulate it. *To be grabbed, forced like a war criminal. Then shoved outside. His war was never over. The violence he witnessed, or committed, or wished he had committed, but did not have the courage, lived with him in that dark basement.*

Maria listened to Wanda. "Her mother was gone again. The entire basement felt black. No windows. In that cold and wet basement, evil funneled through her father, and little Maria was alone with him. After he had bitten, pulled, and pinched her, he held her upside down, and shouted,—." Maria stopped listening after that.

Later, inside her hospital room, Maria heard Wanda again. "Her father forced her to stand at attention while he slammed the base of his palms against her head, then pulled her to the mattress. His urge rose when Maria was at her point of helplessness. She would awake at night seeing her father's triumphant smile when he crawled off her. Then he slept.

"I told her to tell no one of those nights. What's the point? I remembered the girl who told a teacher. She landed in a hospital—beaten by her father. Heard talk of a young lawyer, candidate for county attorney, whose children lived in such squalor that the Pubic Health Nurse reported the family to the out-going County Attorney. After the general election, an assistant county attorney dismissed the charges against his newly elected boss.

"Every night she felt him on her or in her, or just about to ram inside her. Pain and blood. Try to sleep after you're raped. She couldn't.

You couldn't." Maria saw the group's sequential head nods. "Carried it like a tumor. Told to address it, let it go, seek closure."

Maria and Wanda laughed at the therapeutic clichés. Resigned to it, Maria said, "Just gets bigger. Have to learn to avoid it." They laughed again.

Maria listened to Wanda. "On that final night in old town, Maria asked her father, 'Where's mom?'"

"'How ta'hell'm I supposed ta know?' Her father answered through his beer, 'She'd better get her ass home soon with sa' money, or I'll send you out. I'd get fifty bucks for you, and I might give you some crows,' made fun of Maria's mispronunciation, then spit on the floor."

Wanda remembered the gentler details Maria had forgotten. As a little girl, Maria had walked past houses where sun flowed through windows, heat bounced off grass. When a little boy, without averted eyes, asked a child's basic question.

Maria answered, "On the corner."

The boy asked, "What are those?" Referring to the bundle she carried.

"Someone gave me these crows." Maria added, "I love crows."

"They're nice," he said, did not walk away, did not make fun of her "l", "r" speech confusion.

She stood motionless, "You and your parents live here?" They did.

Maria asked, "Together."

"Yes."

"All the time?"

Nodded.

"It must be nice", walked away embarrassed and puzzled.

The little boy smiled, waved.

On Maria's last night, she awoke to the sounds of four adults in the basement house. Hours later, louder voices. Her father raging. Her aunt—drunk and angry. Her mother—drunk and happy. An unknown man stunned. In an instant, the aunt and man disappeared; Maria crawled outside to her mother—curled and wet. Her father inside. Door locked.

"Mom—" Saw her only in outline. "What'll we do?"

"I know what I'm not gonna do. I'm not goin' back in there. What you do is up to you." Her mother's back a slumped question mark, raised her middle finger, continue to walk. Maria hurried to keep up.

Maria hurried after her mother through a series of pick-ups, pick-up trucks, trailer parks, dusty roads. Wore off-the-shoulder dresses in junior high, accommodated Sunday afternoon visits by anxious, pimply boys—brimming with expectations of fulfillment in nearby tree groves. *Then we'd hurry off to another trailer park. Another school. The same. Then, somewhere else.*

Maria had continued to hurry, away from, but always focused toward, those dark nights. Through early mistakes, starts and accelerations, jobs and marriages, made a young girl's promise—years until fruition.

Inside Judy's hospital office, Maria said, "Well, that quieted everyone. Never thought a chair movement could do that." Added, "Wanda and I want to meet with you privately."

Judy, behind her metal desk, shifted with appellate authority, said, "No one-on-ones. No secrets. You must do group. It's hospital policy."

Maria told Wanda, "They'll throw us back into that cauldron every day, until there's a breakthrough and compliance. We'll just agree with them. Cry maybe." Knew if either of them cried, they'd never stop until they ripped in half.

The next morning, in that circle of chairs, Maria awash in folded arms, pursed lips, judgmental eyes, each member thought one thing and mouthed another. Arms, hands, eyes, faces never in sync.

Judy rolled her high-back chair into the circle, shifted forward, her calves tensed. "Maria, you're too comfortable with your anger. Right? It feels familiar to you. Correct? You and your friend, Wanda, are on a well-traveled path of resentment. Am I right? You both think it's a safe path, but it's not. True? You use your temporary physical pain as your crutch. Right?"

Physical pain. Pontificated—as if it's minor. Maria maintained eye contact, needed to blink to stop the burn, refused to give Judy the satisfaction. Maria considered whether to agree, to argue, to allow Judy to slap her with the metronomic broad brush of counselor's insight.

She heard Wanda's comments. *Judy, in her warm-in-winter, cool-in-summer office, drives to lunch in a new car, maintains her waistline at a gym, sports a diamond ring. Yes, I'm positive she knows how we feel, feels our pain, hears what we're saying. Maybe even knows where we're coming from. She knows all the trite balms.*

Maria's pain served as her bookmark into that night on the turnpike. Her third husband, the father of Theresa, his hand on the steering wheel, cleared his throat, said something. Maria laughed. *How many times have I heard his crap?* She usually only registered his voice as a series of blats, it lodged like a clown act. However, he does put food on their table, and he is the father of her child.

However, the father of her child is dating someone ten years younger, someone with no child, someone whose body is younger, tighter, more compliant. And his stories are all new to her.

Maria looked around the group. Judy nodded permission, Maria said, "Me, I'm too tired after working five days a week, then coming home, and working seven days a week for him." She rubbed her eyes, "When he wants me, I fake it, let him finish, smile. He's relaxed. Falls asleep."

That morning her husband announced they were eating dinner at one of the lakeside restaurants in their land-locked state—all with hopeful names like The Kingfisher Inn and Big Island Grill. Inland diners that label themselves island restaurants. Her name for the restaurant tonight was the Long Time No Sea. One of the restaurants built alongside borrow pits from massive interstate highway near water conservation projects.

Maria heard the group rustling, waited for their noise to abate. "Before we went to dinner, all I had to do was go to work, get home, feed the kids, orient the babysitter, get dressed, belatedly remember my husband's instructions, go back upstairs, and put on the shorter dress with the lower neckline, apply a different attitude, and be at the front door smiling and waiting. My husband's job was to drive home from work, park the car, walk in the house, and signal he was ready."

Eyes ricocheted from Maria to floor to wall to window, back to Maria. "That night, my husband got home thirty minutes late and honked the car horn." Maria, her voice unsteady, looked at Wanda, closed her eyes, continued, "He honked. In front of his own house, he honked as if I were some high school slut. Someone only good for the backseat of his car."

Silence. "What did you do then? When you heard the horn?" Judy asked, then leaned back.

"I ran to his car."

"Like that slut?"

Maria swallowed. *What's it matter. Just listen.*

Their dinner consisted of too much Scotch, beer, resentments. Driving back, his monologue began. *Maria laughed. Yes, she laughed. Not some cutsie giggle indicating she thought he was clever. Maria laughed—throaty, contralto—like an adult.*

Maria followed Wanda's guidance, answered, "Because tonight he sounded the way people do just before they're committed. And I was sick of it." Saw blank faces that reminded her of photographs. "He slammed the brakes. The car lunged. Then slowed. Turned. Stopped."

"What happened then?"

Maria heard Judy's question. "I laughed again. A mistake. I knew the script. He'd act angry. I was supposed to respond, make it easy for him to toss me in the back seat. Pretend to resist, fake a struggle, yield. Within minutes, he'd tense, become limp. I'd drive him home, put him to bed."

Wanda talked, while Maria studied the hospital walls, calming shades of green, photographs of scenes seeking to invoke composure, maybe even inspiration. "But hell no," Wanda said, "not tonight. She couldn't just act like a good little girl. Couldn't just do what he wanted. Couldn't follow the script I taught her. She had to act like an adult with a sense of humor. She had forgotten the basics: When a man says he wants a woman with a sense of humor, he really wants a girl who'll laugh at his jokes."

"Anyway," said Wanda, she told him, 'I didn't say anything. Just laughed.' Then he shouted, 'You laughed at me?'"

"No, not at you, at Letterman's jokes. Hell, yes, at you."

His fist hit the side of Maria's head restraint, and her head rebounded. No discussion ensued. No open airing of differences. No active listening. Only the back of his hand across her chest, then his open palm up under her chin, followed by his thumb at her throat, then in her eye. Then pools of red."

The group heard Maria's voice, "He punched at my hands covering my face. That hurts worse than you'd think. A man twice my size pounded me." Maria's eyes narrowed by degrees, then closed, "He pushed me out of the car. Hauled me past the tall grass into an open area. His hands and knees slammed my stomach, then my chest, then—" Maria stopped, grabbed for air, swallowed it, continued, "I thought it was bad before. About every two months, he'd go on a rampage. Accuse me of something, then beat me. Had to cover up bruises everywhere."

Maria heard another group interruption. "Excuse me. You said what? I couldn't hear what you said, I was talking. Say it again." Maria pushed her hands against the chair. Judy repeated herself. Maria responded. "Really, you said it happened years ago, so I should—? What? Let it go? Let it go?" *Screw you.* "Let go and let who? You're kidding?"

She heard their voices, then Wanda's calming sounds. *They don't want to hear about it. They'll interrupt again. Do what I taught you. Repress and comply.*

Maria saw her hospital room as white, the windows moved higher. "Anyway, he jerked up my dress, grabbed my hands, spit on me, after that, an internal hammer, then he tensed and went limp. Rolled over, caught his breath, pulled my blouse off, wrapped his fists, beat the living hell out of my face."

"No interruptions now? No smirks or laughter? No snide comments? No insights? Here, look at her photos." Maria saw no hands reach out for the photos in Wanda's hand. "No? You don't want to look at them. Too much to handle? Too intrusive? Been intruded on, and into, all her life. Take these photos. Look at them. Does it look made up? Overstated? This was a beating. Look at the face. Purple swollen cheeks. The black crust. Swollen eyes, eyeballs full of blood. Color photos. It happened that night. Where's your insightful feedback now?"

The room now all white, the windows had moved closer to the ceiling near the light. Saw her marriages as a series of alcohol, submission, with the fluid of her husbands' assignations dripping over her. Had been beaten into her that she was to blame. Made futile attempts to make herself better. *She tried not to do things that made men angry. Failed. Wondered what did she do to make men treat her that way? If someone had told her, she would have stopped.*

In bed, hours later on the night of her beating, Maria's husband awoke, shouted at their crying baby, "Shut up you blubbering baboon, or I'll chloroform you." Shoved his foot into Maria's thigh, "You, shut her up, or I will."

Maria left the bed. Dried, changed, fed, quieted Theresa, placed her in a carrier. Collected her thoughts. Her choices were basic—chair or knife. Made her decision. No 911 calls. No Help Desk. No 800 number-toll free busy signal. No emergency room visits.

Outside the bedroom door, heard his snoring, crept inside, the door remained open. Stopped, allowed her eyes to adjust, made sure she did not bump anything.

Minutes later, she left the house with Theresa.

Maria, exposed and alone inside that group, noticed the wire-covered ceiling light, heard questions, answered, "What's next? I'll tell you. First, decide when, if, how and why to come back to the house. How to support Theresa." Answered, "Community shelters? Maybe. But that's temporary. Other social programs? Not many of those around anymore."

Maria ignored the movements of someone imitating a traffic cop. "Relatives? Dead. My friend's taking care of Theresa." Maria hesitated, looked again at the movements, "but as good a friend as she is, she's as unstable as her own telescoped tragedies."

As if remembering someone else's life, Maria said, "There's more."

Maria heard another question, assumed a snide demeanor. "There's a thought. Take some time to heal, to be cured. Then I'll be fine. And, after all your help, I'll really be cured."

"No? My mistake, you didn't say that. I won't be cured? You want me to look around. Look around this room. You're telling me I'm by myself. Alone? No group. Only a locked door with a small window." She looked up, heard a voice.

"Say that again, please." Waited. "All the doors are locked. I have to stay. Until when?"

Maria heard another voice, responded, "Until a court declares me sane?"

Silence.

Asked, "But who's going to tell Wanda?"

Twilight Storm in Cochise County

Jeffrey C. Alfier

This August heat could sedate the devil.
My sweat falls onto ground the good book
swears owns us in the end, switchbacks

to chew my heels into bygone bone
even as sky blues to the storm front's
umbral cast. Shadow-rimmed cottonwoods

darken along an inscape of cutbanks
in a wind that cradles the musk of creosote
and shivers softly the shafts of thorns

that sift the ochre billows of dust-devils
dispersed like sentinels. They range over
miles of mesquite that swathe forever

toward foothills of the Whetstone Mountains.
The falling light ravels the skyline
to a loose seam, rain now muttering

its presence like a stranger's voice breaking
into a daydream, torrents soon cutting loose
on my woman's roof, up the valley in St. David.

Her good love is all the luck I've ever found.
She waits just behind her front door, as a moth
plays in a porch light, an angel made of dust.

Provender for an Hermosillo Hunter

Let sweat and dust have all of you, till you meld
into the whitetail's cloven trace. Invincible
heat will still you like a secret.

Be acacia or mesquite, thorn-laced, robust
enough to survive beleaguering light,
the sea of thirst that would drown you.

Hawks glean your intent, drag their shadows
in countersign along cutbanks you crouch in.
A wrong step could envenom your blood.

Spot and stalk. Hesitation is under-kill. Be the desert
burning in your crosshairs. There is space
enough out here, a silence as breathless as yours.

New Church on the Corner

John P. Kristofco

Once it was a garden, then a farmhouse,
an open field when they paved the roads
to put it on the map,
a dry goods, then a market
when a man and woman came
to fill it with the April of their lives,
canned goods, candy counters, apple pies,
long before the woman went away,
the slow decay of cities as they rust,
close their eyes against the dust that shutters windows;
now it is to be the Eden Church
where new paint and the sign outside
await the word of God,
and leathered gray-brown trees
give birth to withered leaves,
faded as the bricks, the door,
abandoned shelves and counters in the store
where children once bought sodas and a Hershey bar,
ate apples from a basket,
read comics while they waited for the bus

St. Kitts

James B. Nicola

The beach too shallow there to dock, and our
liner anchored far off, we shuttled to
dry land in tender boats to romp and spend.
To them, as we came into focus through
the fog, up the ramp, to the taxi queue,
we were undissolved, congealed, like apparitions, evidences of elsewheres,
fulfilling prophecies of yesterdays.

This will be their last year of sugar cane.
Soon they'll depend on faith alone—a faith
not blind but based on decades of experience
of emissaries from another world,
our world, who came to spend, and on reliance
that next year, we shall come and spend again.

Crumbs in the Butter

Kelly Miller

Retinal flash of your dad's sneer as he turns your way after flipping-off your Granny behind her back. His arms thrust upwards. Both middle fingers long white and obscene.

Screw his mother-in-law for feeling inconvenienced by his pant stretchers hanging in the shower. Screw her for sighing and complaining with a half-glance. Screw her for begrudging him this small space while he's still here.

Your dad's pants stretchers. Those metal frames your mom inserted into each leg of his tan work pants and hung to dry in the shower. Half dozen at a time. Ensuring his pants dried wrinkle-free and with perfect creases. Add a bleached cotton tee and dark green shirt. Top it off with a tan cap to tame his copper curls. And you've got the only clothes he ever wore. Work or play.

Don't forget. In your wedding photo your dad is in a suit for you. He is without his hat for you.

The diagnosis came the morning of your high school graduation. Tumors ignored, denied, spread. Your dad failing to show or even mention his swollen testicles to three doctors. Three misdiagnoses. Sciatica, stress, back strain.

Doctor number four shaking his head as your dad tugged up his pants. Held the zipper closed with one fist. Wide-eyed and apologetic like a guilty little boy.

Cancer. Prostate. Just like his father, your mom said. Turning from the huddle she'd made of your brother, your sister, yourself. Turning to light a cigarette. A cigarette is usually a comma. This one. A period. Metallic click of the bathroom door against its latch. Your mom's palms, forehead and deep sigh falling away on the other side.

In the evening you celebrated graduation. An Easter branch painted gold. Rolls of cash tied with ribbons. A small cedar chest for memories.

Nobody wanted cake. The pink champagne stayed corked.

Your dad dying in the middle of your excitement. Graduation, marriage, pregnancy, a new house. Not necessarily in that order.

Before the cancer your dad came home grumpy from work. To clean up and be fed. To disappear inside TV or books. He lured you into reading by leaving paperbacks splayed open on his headboard. By leaving the bedroom door wide so you could watch a novel rise and fall across his belly. *All Creatures Great and Small. The Call of the Wild.* His all-time favorite *Green Mansions.*

On Friday nights, between beers and pulls from a brown-bagged bottle, your dad gave you stories. The only time he'd talk about the war. Never guns or blood or fear. Though you felt them near beneath words he turned quickly from. There was the Italian woman who gave him fresh eggs and a dusty half-bottle of wine. There was the time he and a buddy had to deliver a baby. There was the sad contrast of colorful toys inside crumbling buildings.

On Saturdays your dad laughed and groaned over *Fractured Fairytales* with you. And took you to buy comics and Chiclet gum.

Sunday mornings the whole family piled in the car for country drives. Slowing to note the height of the corn. The heft of the hogs. Stopping to fill grocery bags with fallen pears. Hickory nuts and hedge balls rolling around in the trunk. Cattails bobbing out windows. Cupped in Granny's aproned lap a jack-in-the-pulpit or curly fern your dad dug up for her garden.

Your dad gave you drama every Sunday as he sobered for the work week. It would be nice if he'd made a list, stuck it to the fridge or taped it alongside the bathroom mirror. But you had to learn your dad's rules the same way you learned not to touch fire. By experiencing the burn, the quick blister. And vowing never to touch again.

Remembering. Don't wipe catsup from the bottle neck with your finger. Never leave crumbs in the butter. Always put the toilet lid down. And never bang the back screen. Or leave hair in the sink. Or mumble when asked a question.

Three pm Sunday. Become an expert at small movement. Pin yourself against walls in passing. Do not make yourself a target for his anger. Do not risk the tremble of another god damn it. Or worse, his silent small-eyed stare.

At supper when you reach for the bread don't bump your dad's arm, pull quickly back and send silverware crashing to the floor. This collision of touch and quick withdraw. That sudden bouncing clang. Stiffens his spine.

Wish to skirt the baseboard like a roach in sudden light. But do not move. Freeze. Like in a game of statues.

Don't worry if he throws his half-filled plate into the sink and stomps away. Don't worry. He'll come back for more. Don't worry.

Grow tall enough to be out of the house on Sunday afternoons. Find reasons not to come home until bedtime.

Remember the blessings of your dad's deep pockets. Plenty of change for pizza and ice cream. Towers of Christmas and birthday presents. New bikes. And always cool clothes for school. Forget how embarrassed you were to be dropped off at friends' houses and school dances in that beat up old Chevy. Your dad didn't mind not having a new car. Something shiny and sharp like that red Jeepster he'd bought with his war money. And drove round and round the town square until your mom unknotted her apron, plated her last cheeseburger and fries at the Purity Café, and agreed to marry him.

Don't forget his quiet love for her. Two fingers at the small of her back as she slid into the car. Encouraging her to drive without a license up and down your dusty Iowa backroads. How he loved tossing back the better part of a six pack while listening to her talk. *Love, Artie* written small and tight at the bottom of valentine, birthday and anniversary cards. *Norma* in wide sweeping curves across envelope fronts.

Be thankful your dad lived to see the baby. And thankful for that peek past the slatted blinds of your new house. Your dad squatting beneath the willow in your back yard, pushing aside tears with his thumbs. You knew he was happy for you. And sad he'd never push his granddaughter in a swing tied to the perfect branch of that tree. Be thankful for what you might never have seen looking straight on.

Near the end your dad sleeps sitting up in his recliner. Lying down is too much like the grave. Everyone standing around, shuffling feet.

He cries out sometimes. More fear than pain. Followed by apology. I'm sorry. I must be dreaming. Then. Let me die I want to die I don't want to die.

Hands and faces fussing about. Words staccato notes. Dad. Please. No.

You watch from the doorway. You are your father's baby. Nineteen. With your own baby on your hip. Nothing is expected of you.

Breathe in the sweet clean press of your daughter's skin. Hang on to that promise of clothes and shoes to buy. Pencil scratches on wood-work charting her growth.

Your sister-in-law steps boldly forward. Wide-eyed and unshaken at the arm of his terror. Her voice pitched to soothe and command. Artie, we're gonna get you up for a minute. Okay? We got cha.

Your brother and sister lunging to catch.

Your dad has shit himself. It's okay to say shit. It's one of his favorite words.

They shimmy down his pants in front of the television where the Yankees are losing their lead again in the bottom of the sixth and rain is threatening to fall.

With a firmness that equals safety, your sister-in-law says, Hold him. Like this. Under his arms. I'll clean him.

She coos every step. The way you do when changing the baby's diaper. She can touch him this way. She is once removed. Daughter-in-law. Not a direct part of this body deteriorating.

Your dad dies with a silver cross around his neck. This man who insisted, There's nothing on the other side. When I'm gone just toss me to the hogs.

A nurse at the VA hospital slips the cross over his head a few days before he falls into a coma. She doesn't know to avoid such topics as Death, God, and Afterlife.

She comes upon him in the midst of one of his nightmares. A sea of hell's hot lava. Demons clawing his freckled ankles. Your dad apologizing for crying out and disturbing others.

Never rude to strangers, he lets her carry on about a loving creator and bliss filled eternity. She tells him that even if he doesn't believe, this cross will bring him comfort.

He tells your sister that when the nurse slipped it over his head he thought what the hell...what have I got to lose?

This woman's kindness is not cluttered by proximity. She's not familiar with the god your dad has never believed in.

The god who failed to stop his baby brother from toppling into a tub of scalding water.

The god who set him down at nineteen in the middle of a war with a gun he refused to fire. Then insisted he stay and watch Mussolini hang by his feet outside a petrol station in Milan. Passersby spitting and pissing on the corpse.

The god who trapped him in a factory job he hated. Blackened clothes, and dirt never quite gone from beneath his nails. And when he got the promotion and white hardhat, the alcohol said he hated that as well. The guys he used to work and eat and smoke and bitch with suddenly faking smiles and calling him Sir.

The god who made it impossible to be kind while sobering for the workweek.

This nurse won't know the god who left your dad living for the weekends. When he could push past the back screen. His lunch box under one arm. A six-pack of Falstaff beer beneath the other. Both items tucked, not held.

After the funeral you'll taste black olives for the first time. The one food your dad never convinced you to try will be offered up on the pinky of your sister's amazon blonde friend. Donna, who never knew your dad, who wasn't there for the fear, the mess, the dread, won't ask how you are or try to fix things.

You'll sit with Donna far away from the radio playing a sickly mix of pop and country. Far away from that fake leather contraption with orange dials that the guys at the factory bought for your dad.

Donna tells you about places she's been, things she's done. Wishes, dreams, regrets. She doesn't care if you listen. Casually she winds your curls around her finger as if they were her own. When you say you like her glass bead necklace she slides it over your head. And because she doesn't ask, you tell her one of your earliest memories. I must have been four or five, you say.

Pulled from sleep by thunder and mom's hands taking you not to the basement's safety, but onto the porch to watch the neighbor's roof. Struck and flaming.

Cold gasps of rain and wandering hoses. Excitement thick as smoke. A thing perhaps you could touch. The ends of your fingers sparking like power lines they fear might catch. Dad's fingers red-spidering as he reaches to gather your blowing curls into a fat pony. Mom breathing nearby. An unlit cigarette tight between two fingers. While your brother calls from the street, I'm going to get a little closer.

Granny warning from inside the screen door, Get back here. Do you wanna be dead? Your mom pointing to a small gap between angled police. Over there. Lifting you onto the saddle of her hip. Leaning into the wind and red fire's ash. Dad following close behind.

Shutting your eyes against such brightness. Preferring the play of flame and shadow across your lids. Safe inside a cloud of smoke and Old Spice, Chanel No. 5 and rain.

Unexpectedly Granny is beside you at the curb. Frightened by the storm, she is more afraid to be alone. She clutches her thin robe to her throat. Her long white hair, loosed from its usual bun, flies about and tangles across her eyes.

Your dad gently tames her hair. Lifting strands into a circle formed by his thumb and middle finger. Holding Granny's makeshift ponytail, he points to the rumbling clouds and says, See how quickly the storm is passing?

Chairbed

Dianna Henning

Such ecstasy when the chairs met
face to face and you tucked pillows in,
spread out your blessing blanket,
climbed aboard your life.

From the doorway the hickory straight-backs
looked like school chums
about to knock fists,
but shyly holding back.

Beyond the window screen,
summer's careening birds,
rustle of rabbits and quail
in the desert sagebrush.

Hickory was perfect wood for other worlds,
until the Elders argued chairs
are nothing more than seats,
and took apart what you'd carefully made.

Open Says Me

Joan Frank

Old means the worst of it, everyone's nightmare. Pleating. Saggy pouches. Fecal breath. Upper-arm wattles. High-belted pants, stretch synthetics. Leaking eyes, discolored teeth, lipstick clownlike. Hair where it shouldn't be, no hair where it should. And smells? Don't get her started.

So she can't be *that*. Christ on a cracker.

Hills burnt now, sideways smears at fifty miles per hour. Familiar storefronts. A soft, retro place, the West County. Orchards and vines reach toward the sea. Jars of honey on card tables, dull throbs of gold catching afternoon light, "pay here" scribbled on the shoebox beside them.

She's old enough to avoid stating her age. That reflex—biting down before the number bleats out—arrived fully formed; she can't pinpoint when.

She can remember a time when even *hearing* such a number—her own sum now, of years—made her erase at once, in her mind, that number's owner.

She runs a hand through her short spikes; checks them in the rearview. (Who's to please, besides herself? Women at the gym?)

She's still a good driver. No one needs to know she's lost an inch of height. Never tall to begin with. She wonders for a moment whether she resembles her late tiny mother, who learned to drive in the rock-strewn Arizona desert—a woman so small she'd had to crane up to see over the dash—with herself, little Frannie, jouncing like a ragdoll in the back seat.

No seatbelts back then. Another measure of age.

Still—the same number can give comfort. If she's slept well and emptied her colon and had a serious cup of coffee that morning and a nice salad the night before and avoided booze and used the good shampoo and conditioner—then the world clarifies, glows. Streets, homes, fields—seen how many thousands of times?—press toward her with fresh, fragrant roundness, like new bread.

Also, age makes things simpler. Less confusion.

Bach trumpets from the radio, one of the Brandenburgs, unfurling against scrub-brush, through air rank with hay and manure. Stands of chestnut, birch, blackberries, mostly picked. Blond meadows, dried to trampled stalks. Such a warm, early autumn—unwilling to give way to what it must.

She lets her head fall back against the rest. It makes her arms, holding the wheel, feel longer.

Once, there'd been room for confusion. That doesn't mean when she was *young* young. It means young enough to still be able, in low light, to turn a head or two. Even when those heads belonged to men whom anyone, under any sort of light, would call older.

Old*er*. Not *old*.

God, how we cling to distinctions. *When it's just a conveyor belt. Not a matter of will.* Hilarious. As if you could blame people—prosecute them for failing to stay young and beautiful.

Turn a sharp right, Lolly's e-mail said, *just after the deer crossing sign onto a dirt road.* Frannie glances again at the page, printed extra-big, on the carseat beside her. She can already feel her face tightening into the public smile. Presentation smile, grocery aisle smile, parent-teacher smile. *A face to meet the faces.* Sometimes she feels it stealing over her in bed, in the dark.

Inane American reflex. But that's not where she meant to go.

It's a party. Not fucking Judgment Day.

Bach gives over to Corelli. Sweet, weightless notes like braided light. *Archangelo.* Apt first name. Heated landscape exhales into the car: eucalyptus, mesquite, anise, straw. *This most excellent canopy, the air.*

Nothing more innocent than a party. Thrown by a jolly retired doctor, Zack, who owns a vineyard. Zack looks like Super Mario in a tank top. Drinks his own wine day and night. (Weak as piss.) Complicated second marriage: kids and grandkids from different hookups swarm the place, wearing limp t-shirts bearing slogans like *John Mayall 1982*, streaming through the shambly house. A constant party, even when there's no party. Doctor Zack wanders the place like an old lamplighter, twinkling godfather to them all.

Frannie creeps the car along the rutted road. Scarlatti plumes from the dash; dust plumes behind. Last warmth, November's polleny light. Flanks of eucalyptus nod, jade leaves draping long branches. Beyond the trees, rows of grapevines blanket out and out.

Frannie counts herself one of Zack's friends, though that's a stretch. Frannie's husband, Kirk, once taught an extension class, journalism, to Zack's current wife, Lolly. Forever ago. Lolly wanted to expand her horizons, or whatever new young wives called it. Later, Kirk and Lolly found they exercised at the same gym. Frannie (who belongs to a different gym) gnawed at that for a while, then ordered herself to stop. Lolly and Kirk had nothing in common—Kirk reminded Frannie several times—except temporary sweat. Nothing to say to each other, he'd repeated carefully, except helloing en route to different machines. Often those brief greetings led to an invitation to another party out at Zack's, which always jollified Kirk (who treated every invitation, Frannie pointed out, like a command).

Kirk adored Frannie. She'd never doubted that. And Lolly wasn't disagreeable to look at, but she wasn't drop-dead. Lolly was half Zack's age, was the thing. Zack might be in his seventies, apparently nowhere near dropping dead yet.

It was Kirk who'd dropped dead, gym or no. A stroke, five years ago.

People invited Frannie to their parties when they remembered to.

Say my glory was I had such friends.

Frannie reverses the hatchback onto the soft grass near the house, where many cars will later spawn. She's arrived at exactly the named hour. Two other cars on the grass. She'll look ridiculous if she ventures in there now. Some past part of her—the schoolkid part or the teacher part—can't avoid being on time, which always means too early. What kind of person arrives on time to everything? Kirk used to shake his head. She'd harass him out the door hours ahead, in case of traffic or botched directions. It was her own firewall rage she'd had to pre-empt if they wound up racing in panic for a plane or train: *This was preventable.* But explaining that was too knotty, or maybe plain sick. So she hadn't.

Albinoni now. Adagio—organ. Pensive, deliberate. Circus turned funeral. She punches it off hard and breaks a nail, swears viciously and pushes herself from the car, slamming the door.

Tugs down her jacket, gazing about. *Sadness of late afternoon.* Light softer. Air cooling, sweeter. Sky that deep, sharp, saturated blue, so pure it seems to vibrate. That, and the stillness: a kind of breathing. Rows of vines like neat seams raying out from the house. Chalk-and-pepper smell of turned soil tapping at her nostrils and heart.

All ye know on earth, and all ye need to know.

She turns from the tree-shrouded house, its muffled voices and plate-clinking. The road is dry, packed, pleasant to set feet down upon. She watches her shoes, which lace up through eyelets like oxfords, except they are lightweight, *café-crème*, a dancer's. She wonders if Kirk would have liked these shoes. Probably not. Not *fem* enough. He'd always peeked—gallantly trying to conceal it—at the strappy spike heels on other women, or in store windows. And whenever she saw this—after fifteen years, felt as much as saw—it sank her heart. *You* try walking around in stuff like that, she'd told him. See how it makes *your* back feel. After a time, they knew it best to say nothing at all.

Her steps are noiseless. The vines, recently clipped of their black and green fruit, have begun their annual ebb; leaves chartreuse, crayon-gold. Soon they'll darken to rust and ruby, crumbling like chipped paint, then to flakes on the ground, then to pink powder—pink of cupcake frosting. What's left above ground will be a horizontal network of stripped branches and stems. Jointed, black, brittle, they'll sleep. Some of the skinnier lines reach from stems so weathered and tough they seem ancient. She bends to examine these. Like mummified arms they reach sideways, fibrous, knobby, veined.

The force that through the black fuse drives. Frannie had taught high school English during her working years. Phrases still tickertape through. Doing dishes last night, staring into the opalescent nets of foam: *those are pearls that were his eyes.*

Silence pours into her now, clear and cool. An electric saw whines far away. She stops again, listening. Stillness can be heaven or hell. This silence has no memory, no opinions. A crow shouts, hoarse, flapping from the vines, careening off.

The nerves sit ceremonious as tombs. She steps slowly on.

What are parties anyhow?

Frannie has never understood them. Kirk lived for them. Any version of *fiesta*. He'd said yes to everything; produced numbing amounts of dinner parties. He'd have done so every night if she'd have let him. (She'd always kept extra rubber gloves and scouring pads under the kitchen sink.) They'd fought about it all their time together, barked ugly words. After sulking half an hour they'd get anxious. One or the other would shuffle up and apologize. They'd embrace, kiss. She might weep into his neck, pledge to be more positive. He'd promise to slow the frequency of the *soirées*. Then in days to follow he wouldn't slow them, because he couldn't. She'd suggest, quietly, that he was congenitally unable. Too many people to care about, he'd reply with a wobbly smile; the smile would undo her. Days on the calendar would fill again with ink, and the combat would resume. She'd always wondered, immediately after those fights, whether she might hate herself one day for it.

They could never stay angry, thank God. It made them ill. She might cry a bit. He'd hold her. They'd kiss, laugh. Then she would blow her nose and go make popcorn while he tried to find something good on the Comedy Channel.

They couldn't have known better—unless you factored in some magical prior knowledge. Silly as proposing that the past can resupply itself in the first place. And wasn't fighting with someone finally just a way of saying *Hey, I'm alive over here?*

She watches her feet. A swallow dips past. The vines are still.

Here was another of the zillion things she'd loved about Kirk: she got to co-own his knowledge.

It was a ruinously good deal. She'd never had to do any of the work—never had to be responsible for bar charts and population counts and names of all the kings of France and England, periods of art or politics going back to tar pits. Just by being his mate, she could draw from his wisdom anytime. And because of that, in people's eyes she owned it as fully as he did—though in fact she didn't. Not a crumb. If someone tossed bait—an argument, a comment, a provoking point—she'd just look over to Kirk. He would already be leaning forward, eyes snapping like a birder who's spotted a rare species. In hearty, sensible language he'd begin to lay out the information. People would listen, watching his face. It was like opening a treasure chest. No: like opening Ali Baba's cave door to piles of jewels in glittering pyramids. *Open says me* was how she'd thought the command was pronounced, as a kid. Made sense at the time.

Did it work in reverse? Sometimes. She loved French, and she had an affinity for music. She would coach Kirk when a piece wafted from the car radio: Okay, who is that? His eyes would narrow over the steering wheel. Miles Davis? Aaron Copland? Yes! She'd clap, and watch the pride relax his face.

That face. And the smell, and silky warmth, of his neck. Vanilla, musk, shaving cream. She shakes her head like a horse, walking; folds her arms though it's not yet cold.

The depth and strength of his mind like a supporting wall. A dropped phrase or two from Kirk made her someone better than she could have dreamed of being.

A robin flutters up from the dust, darts off.

While Kirk was alive, she'd wondered what it was going to be like to lose that wall of knowledge behind her. For the wall to vanish.

How would the world shrink—or loom? How much less herself would she feel?

Plenty, had been the answer. Whatever selfhood she may still possess feels more like a membrane. Or so she judges herself these days.

Again with the judgment!

Parties.

She kicks a stiffened ridge in the road, still holding her elbows. They should be called something truer to fact. Snaggle of mismatched people talking, holding drinks. Talkies with drinkies. Tinkies. Tink, a-tink-a-tink. And the tediousness. Holy God. Like auditioning over and over. Stupefying trifles no one remembers. Or else you already know everyone's resumé by heart, and no one has a thing to say they have not said ten thousand times.

So you empty glass after glass. And next day your head is packed with steel wool and your mouth tastes unspeakable.

She'd had this conversation with Kirk all their days. He'd finally shrug and go water the plants.

Drinking, then as now, seemed the only remedy. Next day be damned.

Which it most assuredly is.

If a gig offers music, that's better. There's often dancing at Zack's. There's supposed to be dancing tonight. *The dancers go round, they go round and around, the squeal and the blare and the tweedle...*

She turns and trudges back toward the house.

This party, she notices, doesn't quite match the others. Frannie knows almost nobody this time. But no one she sees—surveying the place—makes her yearn to know them better. What are the laws of attraction now, or even of curiosity? Groups of plumpish women stand together, heads a palette of grays. Some still insist on keeping long hair, parted in the middle—as it was when they were peach-cheeked Renaissance maidens right here in the county, baking bread and brewing yogurt, rosy babies riding on hips. Except now the rosy babies are tall and sweaty and founding consultancy startups, and the women's hair hangs thin and coarse and straggly, like moss. Some have cut their hair like a man's, or in a Dutch-boy.

Behind the women mills a pod of older men. They are retired doctors, friends of Zack's from med school. Wiry. Many are compulsive runners, bargaining against the inevitable with suppressed fury. All of them drinking that useless wine. (Not bad-tasting, but no effect.) Several younger men and women loiter in a separate group: these are the high school math teachers. Teaching high school math is what Lolly still does; they're her crowd—and presently busy, Frannie sees, conducting difficult love affairs. She can read it: protective arms around waists, doleful children clinging to legs. Divorce, multiple homes, sundered psyches.

Oh, if only I could fix that. Fix everything.

Fix. A sigh escapes her. Shortened, maybe, from *Felix*, somewhere along the timeline. *Felicidad. Fixer-upper. Feliz navidad.*

Someone somewhere was happy, once.

Muffled rock music pounds from the basement; light shades into dusk. Kids thread through the adults in a daisy chain, faces grim. What the kids seek, Frannie knows, is something to do. Ah, God. *Don't we all.*

She'll want to hang herself in minutes if she approaches the moss-haired women. She's tried it before—sidling up to the little klatch, face taut with false *bonhomie*. The icepick to the heart while the recitals pile up. Weddings, volunteerism, recipes, golf, gardening, meditation retreats, trips to Cinqua Terre.

If she talks to the aging doctors, they'll think she's cruising them. That happened last time—a sort of heavy-lidded, wry appraising *en masse*; made her want to go take a shower. And one of them had promptly clamped onto her like a terrier. A mirthful Jewish guy, skinny and short. Sadness in this: she'd felt shamed and tired. Yet who could fault trying, while we're alive? Gently, she'd ducked away.

Mostly the doctors will stand and smirk at her because she's not a scientist, which in their lexicon means idiot. That's happened, too.

What *does* she want to hear, then? Honestly?

She wants to hear someone say *I haven't figured anything out. I understand less and less. A mystery, isn't it? Kind of shocking, huh?*

Please. She sends out the silent entreaty like a note to the principal. *Make me behave well.*

But that thinking's not fair. It still posits her at the center of some Frannie-minded universe, some genial, hosting sensibility. As if God were a Normal Rockwell soda jerk, sleepy-eyed but cheerful, ready to assemble the root-beer float of her choosing.

And she'll have to drive home. So she cannot immediately drown thought with booze.

Except she can certainly as hell *soften* thought with booze, this very minute.

She begins opening kitchen cupboards, refrigerator—ah. Single bottle of good ale, high octane. Standing alone in there, brave soldier. She cracks open the bottle; brings the cold brown lip to her own lips. *Mother's milk*, Kirk would gasp after that first icy pull: now she hears his words every time.

Find someone to talk to.

Or why not just slip out this minute? Hop into the car, creep away?

Because a party is Something, Provisionally, To Do. Kirk always set colossal store by that. Made him forget time, briefly. Distraction, above all. *From what?* she used to bellow at him, her cheeks hot. *Why isn't the present ever good enough just by itself? Why is time such an enemy?* And he'd look away, anguished, swallowing the counter-accusation she knew had leapt to his mouth: *What kind of monster are you?*

She's neither sorry nor proud of it now. They were who they were. Like eye color.

Kirk had always been fascinated by this world of wine-quaffing doctors and adulterous high school teachers—so unlike that of his lifer slog to the Op-Ed department of the local daily, where his colleagues, sifting and herding endless Letters to the Editor, got fatter and blander and more florid each year, their stomachs preceding them into a room, their hearts and kidneys and livers commencing revolt—the job where he'd put in the pension-earning time to ensure his wife would be cared for in that unthinkable, unimaginable contingency, her widowhood. And how many times had he gazed at Frannie with a kind of incredulous pity whenever she'd tell him she'd rather do *anything, anything* else than screw up her face, one more time, into the Presentation Smile.

He genuinely could never think that way. A natural extension of his decency. And that was what never failed to cut her up. His decency.

She takes another deep pull of the cold ale, and holding the bottle carefully, makes her way down the old wooden stairs.

Thumping of an overtorqued bassline. Murkish dark, smelling of vinegary wood: wine barrels. Through it, her eyes catch upon a young man who zips around, fiddling with knobs on a bank of machines spread across the wall—a launch center of sound control. Difficult to guess his age. Early thirties? Dark hair, thinning so the white scalp shows. Bit taller than her. Unremarkable build, moving fast between dials and levers, placing silvery stacks of CD's in different slots. He seems to float and alight, a sonic bee pollinating the equipment. She strains to glimpse his face: grinning, but wracked. She can read the grin. Capsized marriage. Loathes himself. Wants to disappear, but has promises to keep.

Yet the music he's chosen, amazingly, fills her chest with sweetness. Strange, marvelous sequences. Sam Cooke. Stephen Stills and Manassas. *What do we do, given life? We move around.* Fred Neil. *I've been searchin for the dolphins in the sea.*

The Fred Neil makes strips of skin ripple from her neck to the crown of her head.

But he seems so young. How can he know this stuff? She backs deeper into the shadows of the great wine barrels against the wall, trying to become part of the furniture. Tables with dishes of fruit, dishes of chips. More kids race past. More people tumble into the room. A man seats himself at a drum-set near the equipment and begins to noodle; a half-bottle of tequila within reach, a microphone up front.

She drinks, watches. The ale loosens a tight band around her skull. Busy-bee Man seems to know every word of every song. Sometimes he lopes to the microphone and leans toward it with several others to wail a chorus: she tries to identify his voice in the racket, but it's impossible.

She has scraped up her nerve, and spoken to him.

She's a harmless old widow, for fuck's sake.

Emboldened by ale, she has tapped him on the shoulder, thanked him for the music and shaken his hand while he paused, polite, puzzled, in the kitchen doorway.

She's told him her name and spoken of New York, of all things, because she's assumed that's where he's from. Even as the words issued from her mouth she was thinking *what am I saying?* But he'd smiled (backlit by the kitchen, a blur of people bearing cups, plates). His smile was tentative, sad, and the few words he'd uttered—as if his throat wanted clearing—she could hardly hear. His last name sounds Italian. She can imagine him wearing the white paper cap and blood-smeared apron, darting around behind a glass counter stacking translucent slices of meat, slamming fat pickles into wax paper, yelling. Except he works in computers, commutes to Silicon Valley—though he was indeed born in the East, New Jersey. Most all of us come from there at some point, she'd told him brightly. *What kind of asinine thing was that to say?* He'd had nothing to add, and now she feels a bit raw, certainly foolish.

Then someone asks him to open a bottle; he turns and disappears into the kitchen.

She forgets his name at once.

Her eyes comb the thickening crowd and locate Lolly, whose moon-face has already turned into pudding. Lolly's petite, slender—all those workouts—and even that piss-weak wine has gone straight to her. Lolly once fell asleep sitting at a dinner table, with Frannie and Kirk seated on either side of her. Head dropped, eyelids flumped. It had made Frannie think of the Doormouse, and struck her as wondrously free: a child's freedom. Who is able to slip from the straitjacket of consciousness so guilelessly anymore—drink or no?

Now Frannie takes Lolly's arm. Who is that guy? Frannie points to the young man, who has resumed fastening himself like Spider Man back and forth along the wall of dials and levers. The music's gone to jazz. Mose Allison. *Oh now a young man—ain't nothin in the world these days.* Joe Williams. *Well all right; well okay; uh-you win: I'm in love with you.*

Lolly's pudding face smooths and brightens as she follows Frannie's finger. Oh that's *Vinnie*, she says, her eyes misting, as though she were identifying a beloved pet.

He certainly *could* be the family pet, Frannie thinks. Probably is. She tips the bottle, drains her ale.

If I'm going to be your man, pretty mama won't you take me by the hand—

So tell me about him. She faces Lolly, standing close to be audible.

Lolly, dimpling, looks past her, still watching Vinnie as if reviewing tender, intimate memories. Briefly, Frannie wants to slap her. The noise in the basement intensifies.

He's separated, Lolly shouts, still watching him. From his wife. They have two little kids.

Frannie feels a small piece of interior turf sag.

Lolly smiles on, blissfully. A lady Buddha, Frannie thinks, studying her. Or maybe an opium eater. Nothing seems to make Lolly sad or serious, even when she talks about sad and serious things. Maybe whatever lives inside Lolly is actually always sleeping, a true Doormouse, thumb-sized and curled up, dozing on and on.

Van Morrison follows the jazzmasters. Vinnie has sprinted to the microphone to pose his head alongside two other heads. *You, maaah—brown-eyed girl.* Sprints back to the wall of machines, holding silver CD's to light, squinting at them.

How old? Frannie yells.

What? Lolly puts a hand behind her ear.

Frannie cups her own hands around her mouth and moves closer to Lolly's ear, which smells of violets.

How old are the kids?

Young, says Lolly. Three, four.

Ah, God, murmurs Frannie.

What? shouts Lolly.

I said I'm sorry, yells Frannie. It's awful to hear that.

Lolly nods and seems to grow solemn a moment—or as solemn as Lolly can look.

He visits a lot, she yells.

Frannie grasps, through Lolly's bawled syllables, that Vinnie lives apart from the estranged wife and kids. Pays for everything while moldering in some bare-assed apartment across town with probably a petrified burrito and single jar of horseradish in the refrigerator. Frannie's eyes stop seeing the sardonic doctors and aging Renaissance maidens and watch instead her mind's projections, fanned in smooth succession: the young man pressing the doorbell at his wife's front door like a salesman. The Sunday morning cooking projects, batter or jam sticky underfoot. The outings, punctured or rerouted. Someone drops her ice cream. The Exploratorium is closed for remodeling. The lines extend too long outside the albino alligator exhibit at the Academy of Science to offer any hope of entry. The cries of *DaddyDaddy* fore and aft, of *Mommy lets us do this all the time*—words that feel to him like the cigarette burns he deserves. The clipped sentences and contemptuous glances from the woman he once adored—no doubt still very pretty, perhaps stunning, perhaps killer beautiful. Perhaps he still has sex with her—in fact of course he still has sex with her unless he's getting it elsewhere, which his own guilt probably precludes—and so having sex with the estranged wife must slice things up with a surgical saw: blood-spray of helloing and goodbying.

Especially if the wife is already having sex with some other boyfriend.

Dear Lord. Frannie feels like she's smashed face-first into an invisible sliding glass door. Her nose has gone a little numb. Drink does that.

Before she leaves she has given Vinnie her card, on which her e-mail address is printed. She has told him she sings in the local community chorus, that a holiday concert is coming in two weeks, and that she'd love it if he showed up.

Why has she done this? Why has she let this little geyser of information spew at him? He'd taken her card, his face voided by a spasm of alarm, as though he'd just been fed fried ants and told what he was eating while chewing them. He'd nodded twice, mutely, mouth stretched in a polite rictus. And so she is startled when, a week later, a message pops up on her computer screen.

Vincente Vivione, reads the bold typeface in the "From" column. *Vincente.* Old style. But what kind of name is Vinnie? A gangster name. Television. The fellow who comes home to eat meatballs and drink chianti in his undershirt after a long day of murdering people. Maybe Vinnie has renamed himself. Reinvention. People do that here all the time. A sort of personal WPA.

Aging herself again.

Tell me again where you're singing, reads the message, *what day and time?*

She eyes herself in the full-length mirror. Black is the only color she feels safe in. Trim, yes. Youthful, no. The woman in the mirror looks like the kind that escort retired husbands into casinos, *coiffe* bouncing alertly. She frowns at the mirror.

Outside, the fig tree nods in the rain, filling the window with green-gray light. Kirk planted it; now it threatens to unearth the house. Frannie lets her eyes rest upon it, wishing she were the tree. A life of green on gray, of rainwater. A life of stately turns—as long as no one chops you down, or drags you out of the ground with chains.

She looks for her coffee: by the telephone. The telephone no one uses, that she hates. Kirk never hated it the way she did, because for Kirk the caller might be bearing gifts: an event, an invitation. He'd grow agitated when it rang, bound into the room and halt before it, stare at it like it was a bomb. She'd insist they let the machine pick up first, to see if it was anyone worth speaking to. So Kirk waited through the recorded greeting (her measured voice), then for the caller to speak. Some horrible part of her enjoyed the way he suffered during those waiting minutes. He'd stand there, face cocked toward the machine like the RCA dog, tensed for whatever the inchoate world was about to drop into their voicemail. Neither of them owned a cell phone then, and she seldom uses the one she keeps now.

She takes a sip of coffee: tepid. Nothing stays hot long enough. She is more nervous than she can make sense of. The holiday concert is a yearly tradition, routine, comfortable. But not this time.

Worse: she's slept badly. The inevitable need to urinate some-where around 3:00 am, followed by the cavalcade of thoughts. She'd taken a sleeping tablet, desperate to lose consciousness—never mind the tablet came from the health food store—knowing its groggifying effects would spill over into waking time, which they have. Thought and memory swirl like broken images on a digital screen. She's drunk strong black coffee, which has succeeded in making her tremble without restoring clarity.

Worse, it is raining. Hard and steady, a sound like many small animals running over the roof. Sky and day dark as dusk. A car sluices past, spraying. No one else seems to be alive or moving, or even crawling about.

She hears, through the window, a single duck's call. *Waack.*

Tell me about it. She feels like one of those cat photos on Facebook, whose glare invites the viewer to fuck off. No attention span lately. Not even for Facebook, which lately to her resembles a series of autographs on the plaster cast of someone's broken arm.

Her stomach hurts from the coffee, but she's too unnerved to eat. The velvet silence of the house listens, and waits. That silence has all the patience in the world. Kirk never had patience, though he'd tried. He'd step out onto the front porch and sit on the plastic chair while she finished whatever delayed her—the final makeup or change of earrings, the grabbing of a sweater or bottle of water or apple. She knew he'd thought these last-minute fiddlings psychotic, but the needs just seemed to surface at the last minute. Or her brain was slower. Both.

What is she after, in this young man's regard? Dear God, nothing sexual. Unthinkable, horrible. None of that *Roman Spring* nonsense. No, it had to do with—some weird affinity. Some strangeness in common. Lone wolfness? Maybe he thinks her a kind of mentor. Guidance. Ho, what a rip-roaring mistake. Even if that's what everyone presumed of her, while she taught. *A face to meet the faces.*

She can herself remember assuming, long ago, a magical wisdom, a *savoir vivre*, about certain older people. She'd also assumed

they'd been born that way. Also, born at whatever age they happened
to then be. Why can't she remember who they are?

Christ help us: *who they were.*

She can splash cold water into her eyes for the dozenth time.

She can rehearse. She can run harmonies while waiting for the
hour to lock into position. She can make sure the porch light's on before she drives off through the rain.

She sheds her heels. Tramps in black tights to the front room.
Arranges herself side-saddle on the windowseat and, looking out at the
vacant, wet street, begins to hum.

The carols' bell-tones always fill her eyes. *Wexford. Holly and
the Ivy.* Non-holiday pieces, too. *Eli's Comin'. Hurry Sundown. I'll
Never Hear Bells.* Melodies like currents, pushing away everything
that is not them.

*My seed is sown now, my field is plowed; my flesh is bone now,
my back is bowed—so hurry sundown; be on your way, and hurry me
a sun-up—on this beat-up sundown day!*

Prickling skin on arms and legs.

Unable, suddenly, to sit still.

Jumps up, stalks from room to room, hand to chin, staring at
objects as if they might speak. In the kitchen she stops before the piece
of paper on the table with the felt-tipped marker beside it: shopping
list. Always the same. How Kirk had laughed at these. Archeologists,
he'd hooted, would decide the species had never progressed. Year after
year. *Diet ginger ale. Raisin bran. Salad dressing. Fruit, tofu, popcorn. Library.*

Stillness of the house, windows silver with rain. She wants to
peel off her skin, swim laps, scrub the bathtub.

No: Lock the doors, crawl into pajamas, under the covers.

Why am I doing this. What was I thinking?

You know your song choices kind of knocked me out, he is telling her.

He has found her standing, for air, near the cafe's side entrance.

He's holding a coffee, foam on it. She clasps her cup of herb tea. Roastarama is packed with post-concert celebrants, pushing into its usual crowd of twentysomethings. Dreadlocks, rings through flesh, smells of wet dog. Clothing, despite the rain, looks dusty and biblical. Christmas lights scallop the walls. Smells and sounds competing: espresso, patchouli, damp hair. Periodic whine from the coffee machine; tuneless chords from someone's acoustic guitar.

She hadn't been able see the audience while they'd sung. White stage lights had obliterated everything beyond Mimi, the dwarfish, ageless, freckled choirmaster in gypsy skirt and peasant blouse at center-front. Mimi used to work at a Waldorf or Montessori school—Frannie can't remember which, or when she switched to choir direction; maybe it was just a tidier version of the same thing. But Mimi still exuded that buoyancy: *C'mon kids let's all run up the hill together holding hands right now.* Curly brown hair, upper-arms like full purses—poised aloft for the downbeat.

A *nice midge-modge* Kirk would have called her chorus: young, old, ethnicities. All smiling at Mimi, Mimi smiling back, smiles blizzarding the joint: you'd think their faces would ache. But the whole set-up functioned like hypnosis—one reason Frannie still loves it. *Mimi's face: no other. Mimi's face: the song list, Mimi's face: the pitchpipe.*

Then the bottomless silence as Mimi's arms fell, and lifted.

Forty mouths opened, inhaled. *My seed is sown now, my field is plowed—*

Mimi invited the audience to join the singers here afterward; a surprising number have shown up. Vinnie approached just as she was stepping away from the drinks pick-up. She's thankful the place is so crowded. No girl here seems to turn Vinnie's head, though some, she guesses, qualify as pretty. Combat boots, lace petticoats. When they pass they leave a wake of cheap weed and body odor.

She needs a real drink. Longs for it. Longs for two drinks simultaneously. But the cafe does not serve alcohol. No doubt this was Mimi's wholesome idea. Frannie wraps both palms around the hot tea like it's an offering. She wants to say to Vinnie, *Why are we talking to each other?*

Instead she says, Thanks for the compliment. From you, it means a lot.

He cocks his head, as if needing translation.

Fuck. Has she already sounded as though she were making an overture?

I mean—she stammers—your playlist. At Zack's party. I couldn't believe my ears. It was—well, it was fabulous.

His face relaxes. It does not appear so stricken tonight as it had at Zack's.

Music: the first language. Maybe the last.

How did you *know* all those songs? she asks.

He opens his free hand (coffee in the other): I grew up listening to radio. Stole all the time I could. You know what's weird? (He leans close enough that she can smell his cologne, a tolerable citrus, and she notices that his eyelashes stick out straight instead of curling, like wee paintbrushes.) Something I haven't thought about in years? My mom bought me a transistor radio when I was little, an old-fashioned cheapie that got its power when you clipped an alligator clip to anything metal. I thought that thing was magic. Learned everything from it. And my folks never had to hear!

They thought—he adds, laughing—the music wasted my time, made me lazy. Since all I wanted to do was be left alone to listen.

This is the most Vinnie has spoken to her since they met.

But you're so young, she says, and makes herself look at him when she says it, though her face heats damply. How do you know such a wide range?

He smiles, pleased. I listened to those stations that play the stuff from—way back. From the very earliest. Even the blues kings.

(He has not said *oldies station*, she thinks. That's sensitive.)

Then an impulse.

So did you love *Oh Girl*?

He bobs his head. That song killed me. *Killed* me.

Then he looks at her almost shyly. I sort of adopted it as the theme song of my life for a while.

Something warm opens in her chest—though at the same time a ghost-question flits through: what girl had he once implored not to leave him? His ex-wife?

What about Left Bank? she asks.

He puts a palm forward, like a traffic cop's halt. Please. *Pretty Ballerina*? A dream. A miracle.

She feels for a moment as if she might levitate an inch or two. This was what Kirk called *a feel-good war*.

Vinnie lifts his cup, toasting her. *Ain't No Mountain High Enough*, he says.

The first one, right? Marvin Gaye?

Well of *course* Marvin Gaye.

Made me cry every time, she says.

Me, too!

(*He cried? He's admitting to me that he cried?*)

She doesn't pause.

Runaway, she says.

The smile broadens. Aw, yeah. Del Shannon. Sweetest thing.

His brows lift: *Every Day.*

For an answer she starts to sing, as he nods in time: *It's gettin closer, goin faster than a rollercoaster—*

Immediately she begins another: *Oh, raindrops—so many raindrops—*

He's in: *It feels like raaaindrops—*

They sing together, looking sideways at each other like a lounge act: *Falling from my eyes, falling from my eyes.*

Nobody can hear in the clamor: *There must be a cloud in my head! Rain keeps falling from eyes—Oh, no, those can't be teardrops, cause a man ain't supposed to cry—*

Hard laughter follows, helpless. The cafe roars on; no one pays the least attention. Finally they calm down, staring at their cups. She feels empty in a more pleasant way than she can remember.

It's a tribe, she says, wiping an eye.

He looks up, also pleasantly vacant. Sorry?

Types who know this stuff. Country of its own, you know? Sovereign State of Music. Border patrol, language, postage stamps. Coins. The works.

He considers this. Yeah. Guess so, he says uncertainly.

Oops. Slipping away. Catch him.

So what's going on with you these days? She tries to sound offhand. I know you're, um—on your own. Lolly told me.

She did, huh? His face reassembling, as if to remember where his car is parked.

But that's all, really, Frannie says quickly. You see your kids a lot?

Idiotic question, she thinks, *but too late.*

His face morphs: phony beaming. A real estate agent.

Yup, yup, I see them all the time, he says, examining what's left of his coffee. They're great.

He takes a theatrical slurp.

She stares at him. *Great?* He can do better than that. What is *great*, but the tawdriest red light? Great means *I'm lost, I'm a mess.* But remember—vulnerability got men killed once. Same as any lame or injured animal. Men have to keep themselves puffed up. She remembers Kirk saying sadly, long ago, *it's hard, being a man.*

Well—that's good then! She nods busily, like some sort of deacon in a greeting line. And the kids are fun?

Real estate face: Oh, awesome, they're awesome. We have the greatest time.

Jesus. Much too much *great. Awesome* was no friend, either. She shifts her weight, glad she's near the half-open door, inhaling streams of cool, rainy air.

And are you—some kamikaze urge makes her say it—are you seeing anyone?

Dinosaur word, but she doesn't know the current one. Bonking? Hooking up?

His eyes widen. Seeing? Oh! Yeah! My girlfriend. I've got this new girlfriend. A very cool lady.

He says, blushing: At least, it seems good so far!

She blinks at him.

Your girlfriend, she echoes stupidly.

And where, um, where is your girlfriend tonight?

His face swivels, touring the room, still smiling, to scan the deafening scene.

Here! he says, swiveling. She's around here somewhere. We came together tonight, to hear you sing.

Wow, Frannie says. Wow. That's really—that's really something. That's really—*great* (the word plopping out like a toad). That's just—*great.*

He's standing before her: affable, attentive, awaiting more interview questions.

Interview. Of course, interview. He has asked nothing about herself.

Maybe Lolly already pre-briefed him, so he fancies he knows all there is to know. *A lonely widow.*

Frannie looks around. Awareness has begun to infiltrate, picking up speed.

He'll want to introduce you.

She starts gabbling like a crazy person.

Hey, you know, it's actually time for me to head on out of here—*why is she sounding like a cowboy?*—I almost forgot, I've got this—I've got this *thing* I'm supposed to be at right now, this very minute. (*Thing?*) I promised them, actually. They'll be worried about me. (*Them? They?*) Look, it's been great (*dear fucking God*), just *great* talking with you; would you mind (shoving the teacup at him), would you mind bringing this back over there for me? I'm already late—but really, thank you so much, really, take care now! See you!

One foot in front of the other. The morning cool but muggy, hazy. A few walkers in both directions, dogs on leashes, bicyclists.

It hurts to think.

She can remember most of it. She can remember driving herself home, all the car windows open—the rain had stopped, and a gauze-white moon peered between louvers of cloud. She'd sprinted from the car, scooped the mail, rushed in, leaned back against the slammed-and-locked front door. *Shewww.* Hopped to the bedroom pushing the shoes from her feet with each heel, kicking them away. Wrenched off her clothes; flung them from her as if they were leeches. Stood under a hot shower, head bowed, trying to erase the last image carouseling in her head: Vinnie's face, all pink flusterment, expecting Frannie, who could be his mom, to cheer.

She'd dried herself savagely, moisturized wantonly, shook on the soft old pajamas. In the kitchen, riffled through mail: a flyer for hearing loss. *These new devices have conquered the annoying feedback and whistling problems of previous-generation hearing aids!* Yanked open the fridge; banged it shut so roughly the whole machine rocked. Jerked open a cabinet. Poured long quantities of Cuervo Gold into her diet ginger ale and sat watching late-night television, eating popcorn and drinking very fast. How easily the Cuervo and ginger went down! How had she missed that combination before? And how sparkling the shows' hosts and guests—even the bimbos! Savoring the world's absurdity together. *We few, we happy few.* She laughed aloud at the jokes, scattering bits of popcorn, and returned to the kitchen for refill upon refill, still laughing: warmed, charmed, at ridiculous amounts of peace with everything, not noticing her nose going numb.

This morning, staring into the beaker of syrup-strength coffee, her skull felt leaden, her mouth like something died in it. Her veins seemed to be pulsing toxins.

Had she behaved last night? She'd drunk nothing till she got home. Had she been an ass?

Did it matter one slice of a good goddamn?

Her mind, imbecile parrot, chose this moment to commence singing. *So hurry sundown; be on your way, and hurry me a sun-up—*

She pounded a fist on the table. Her fist reported instant pain. She groaned. Fuck's *sake*.

For hangovers, there are two options. Swim or hike, at frenzied pace, for at least an hour.

She used to take this walk—around Clement Park's man-made lake—every week with Kirk, who was much faster but stopped, at intervals, to wait for her. (Yes. *He kindly stopped for me.*) You've got an eighteen-year-old's legs, she would tell him, breathless as she caught up. And he wants them back, Kirk always replied. She walked like a Monty Python skit, elbows working, both herself and Kirk glistening with the slimy, poison-smelling sunscreen they both hated but that she made them use. She'd occasionally wondered, during those walks, how it might feel one day to have to do them alone. Some far, faraway day.

Why was I not made of stone, like thee?

*Oh—just—shut—*up. *Just shut up until an hour has passed, and a lot of sweat with it.*

She lengthens her stride, following the dirt-and-gravel along the creek.

A small bridge crosses that creek, a bridge over which, every working day of the year, a miniature train passes—shiny red, the kind in which exhausted adults (their squirmy charges in laps and arms) sit in midget passenger cars, glad for the chance to sit down and not have to *generate* anything, just to point at the plastic elves and toy cabins stationed at toddler-eye level as the contraption huffs along. *Ding ding*, goes its bell. That's the prelude. The guide—a teenager doing the job for extra coins—recites a script, blurry over the terrible mike, warning that the train's whistle must blow to scare away the monsters living under the bridge. The guide asks the kids to scream, loudly as they can, to help do the job.

When Frannie began with Kirk, she'd been disarmed by the ritual of the whistle and screaming. Later the sounds saddened her. Now they almost anger her. Marching along, sweating, she hears the loudspeaker hawking itself awake.

The adenoidal voice—incomprehensible over the crappy mike— lifts in pitch to prepare the tots for the whistle, and to encourage their screams...*mur mur mur mur MUR MUR MUR MUR!*

A pause. Frannie stops, presses fingers against ears. Passing walkers eye her with mild amusement.

WHOOO-WHOOO, AUGGGGGGH!

She unplugs, walks on.

Why does the sound claw at her now? It's not about wanting children. She is decades past that and—cliché, but true—has had thousands of them, in her students. It's more that the sound now makes her envision a fast-forward stupidity evolution. Wave upon wave of kidlets tumbling to shore, scrambling over the land like an infestation. Grown in two minutes. Every year, macaroni-and-cheese flesh fell away to reveal cheekbones, jaws, chins. Soon crow's feet, frown lines. But no one got smarter.

A handful of souls came back or wrote letters, thanking her. But too many just *clogged things up* after that, their heavy bodies

and inextricable devices, their valleyspeak, their self-immersed, wit-
less lives.

Oh, give it a break. You're no better.

She holds a forearm behind her back, staring at the terraced
rocks as she huffs through the manzanitas. The air is still. A baby
lizard streaks across the path.

Her eyes follow. *Zzssst:* a single, panicked zip to the brush, where
the lizard disappears. So infinitesimal she's hardly seen it. She stops,
panting; stares at the dry leaves where the moving spot has vanished.

A creature of the earth. Asking nothing. Following genetic laws,
being born, living, dying.

She hears the engine whoot farther away, followed by the chorus
of shrieking.

Something Kirk said, scratching at her.

Everything had to start out somehow.

Usually badly, he'd added.

Hands to hips, panting, she looks up through the branches.

Waves upon waves. *Including Vinnie. Including me. And all
who came before us, and all who follow.* And someone—many some-
ones—would have once dismissed her girlhood self as a moron inter-
loper. Ignorant plasma. Non-useful use of space and matter.

Kirk used to say of the foolish young: *they don't know they
were born.*

No one does, at first.

Some take longer than others.

She steps to her place at the end of the line, under a sort of portico.

Cooling sweat makes her pull her jacket close. Families have
brought their very young, who stare in wonder at the glitter of red and

green tinsel framing the ticket window. She stands behind the grandpa with twins; in front of him a Mexican lady cradles a sleeping infant while holding a preschooler's hand. The kids—anticipating Something Large—are subdued, piping an occasional question or soft whimper.

There are people who get up in the morning and cross a room / and open a window to let the sweet breeze in / and let it touch them all over their faces and bodies.

She holds her purse with both hands, like a guest at a church social.

When she hands the ticket-taker her money, he checks behind her.

Just you? he asks.

Happy Holidays to you too, she says.

She lowers herself onto the bench in the little car—trimmed with colored lights—the scale of everything so shrimpy that seated grown-ups find their knees crowding their chests. She waggles her fingers at the baby with white feathers for hair who faces her from the car ahead, wobbling, gaping popeyed over its father's corduroy-jacketed shoulder: two fat baby hands hooked there, fingers like tiny udders.

The baby's face seems permanently stunned, its lips wet, open. Its eyes never leave her face.

I know exactly how you feel, buddyboy. Kind of shocking, isn't it. Clutching her purse in her lap, she rights herself with the others as the cars at last jolt to life and shudder forward. She'll know when to plug her ears. Maybe she will even try a scream or two. So when the cars begin to move, and the guide's voice honks through the bad mike *Welcome, everyone!* she can inhale deeply, fill herself with the chill air, the lights, the chug-chugging, the bell, the astonished face watching hers.

The Frequency of Higher Registers

Jayson Iwen

In the highest earthly limits
Before the splattered bathroom mirror
Caressing the trigger again
We have all been there

And learned nothing every time
Of a desperation so fine
Nothing more need be said
The moment the tree turns to air

Before the bristle of satellites
Before even the razor of thought
Unbalances atop a parking ramp
A hundred thousand million times

Awoke to our next mother's cries
It knows no needs
Nothing, in fact, is all that can be
There, there, there

Love #9

I sit on an upturned five-gallon bucket
on the frozen waste of a lake bright enough
to burn the sight from my head, but I focus on the black
hole in the ice, and the filament of line piercing it.
Through the line I feel the depth of the body
beneath me and the life that passes through it. One
convulses in the snow beside me, then lies still,
gills fanning, one eye in the snow, the other
on me. Love, I do not want to be
one with you. Like hatred, desire requires
us to be others, so we can draw forever
closer. Thought is the price we pay for this.
I reach beyond my self into what
I imagine, so I can feel what I feel
is not me. And haul up company.
The pike is stiff now, frozen in the vicious arc
of passion his body assumed in its final act
of will. I try to travel light on the surface
of the world. I send back more than I take.
Please, do not do the same to me,
my Love. Make me the precious many you take.

Love #9

Travel heavy on me, and leave nothing
but your self behind, nothing but the shapes
we take in the snow.

Traveling North From Ashland

Sandra Rokoff-Lizut

For Jorge, who crossed the desert at 14.

Low-lying
ribbons of fog
circle the mountain
settle at its base
freeing treetops.
A piney island
appears.

Now and again
a certain image
scent, whisper
surrounds me,
loosens
knots of routine
and I too float free.

In Praise of Slowing Down

Matt Schumacher

How worthwhile to slow down
and know the alpenglow,

as elk cross Lolo Pass
just past our headlights

into twilight shadows.
Slow down and you

might find wild blackberries,
their swollen ripe beads glistening

beneath leaves and thorns,
find sweet, soft seeds adorn

the gravel road to Zigzag Mountain.
Since slowness slips us glimpses of the deep,

spotted bells of pink, spiked foxgloves,
small steeples which seem suddenly

filled with doves, or thrills us with
the sulphur shelf's yellow-orange frills,

regalia for fallen logs, heretofore unknown
heroes of forest folklore, and frees our sight

to light, butterfly-like, on Lost Lake,
exquisite in the distance between dense trees,

it makes humankind more humane
and mindful. Slow down. Please.

Cougar Dreams

Scott Parker

Sandprints

I can trace my interest in cougars to the morning of my first wedding anniversary. Sandy and I were celebrating on the coast. The day before we'd driven south from Lincoln City, down Highway 101 along the water, passing through alternating clear blue skies and thick gray-white fog that chilled and dampened us down to our socks on fifteen-minute intervals as if the ocean were inhaling-exhaling right through us. We checked into a hotel in Florence as the weather finally committed to *bad*: fifty degrees, rainy, blustery. This was August, I should add. But in the morning, as I drank coffee, stared as always into the fog, and read about the destructive force of all the plastic we've put in the ocean, the summer sun burned through enough moisture that I could by 10:00 see the ocean 100 yards before me.

Invigorated by this turn, Sandy and I loaded up the car and aimed south for the Oregon Dunes National Recreation Area, the morass of sand sprawling almost forty miles from Florence down to Coos Bay. This immense stretch of sand, the largest such stretch in North America, is the result of millions of years of wind, sun, and rain erosion on the Oregon Coast. Think Saudi Arabia squeezed between a lush dense forest and world's biggest ocean, or think of *Dune*, which was inspired by these dunes.

By noon we were there and the clouds were gone. I threw my shirt down with my flip-flops and ran madly up the first embankment falling forward and flailing sand wildly about. Atop that first rise, I folded at the waist as the crisp ocean air blew as much salt onto me as my sweat took out of me. My legs ached from strain as my feet sunk into the sand, my chest ready to burst into the atmosphere. Sandy was walking and still had half the climb left. I faced west and was reminded how immense this place is. The thin blue line of the Pacific drew itself flat and thin above the thick ever-changing crests of sand rolling from beneath my feet all the way it seemed to forever. I'll never reach that water, goddamnit, I thought with delight.

When Sandy appeared at the top, we goofed around, took pictures, filmed a video of me climbing and falling down a near-vertical embankment, heard, then saw, dirt bikers and felt righteous hostility toward them. Sandy was content to walk slowly over the sand waves like a desert wanderer. I was hyper. I had to get to the highest point. Each bump compelled me forward to the next. We agreed I'd run ahead and around and such and come back to meet her at a designated tree amidst a nearby valley.

As my outline from Sandy's perspective diminished and eventually disappeared, she must have had opportunity to survey her surroundings. Prone to worst-case-scenario thinking, she would have quickly identified her vulnerability: alone in a valley, high covered ground all around her. Anything could be watching her now, and she couldn't see it, and she couldn't escape. She was surrounded by miles of sand.

And where was I? Right where she figured I'd be: running off in carefree search of adventure, pursuing my intrapsychic Manifest Destiny. Exploring and conquering and all those heroic clichés I can't help but be drawn to.

By the time I decided Sandy must have been running low on patience and circled back to meet her at the tree, she was less bored than convinced of her imminent death.

While I was chasing the horizon, Sandy was moving slowly and carefully observing her surroundings, the ground beneath her feet. The tracks she found were too big to belong to a common small mammal (raccoon, squirrel, opossum, skunk, etc.). They could have been from a dog, but something about them was undogly and they weren't parallel human tracks. Could they be cat prints, she had wondered and soon affirmed for herself. The terrain really appeared dangerous to her now. The high ledges—if she were a cat, that's where she would lie in ambush, and given the prey in the area it was she she would stalk.

She told this to me with sincerity and full vulnerability. *Absurd!* I thought (and probably said). I—walker of dunes, hiker of trails, adventurer among men—knew this land and knew that big cats didn't come around there. I mean not now anyway, not at this time of day, amidst this noise. "It was probably just a raccoon. Show me these tracks."

On the walk back to the car we didn't find the original tracks that Sandy had seen. Before we got to them we found a fresher set. Big and ominous. The sand was caving in already around the edges, but these prints were calm and evenly measured, each wide and menacing. Whatever left these prints was scared of nothing. We debated following them for all of two seconds, but it wasn't worth losing our marriage over, so I agreed we'd hurry back to the car.

Later, safely on the internet, I began my research into the cougars of Oregon. One of the first things I learned was that their habitat is as varied as nearly the entirety of North America and currently includes all of Oregon, including the Dunes. I'd been visiting the Oregon coast thirty years by then and had heard not a word about cougars in the area. Something else I've learned is that it is a common misperception of people who live among cougars to think they don't.

So, was Sandy stalked? No. Did we cross cougar tracks? Probably not. But probably not is not definitely not. And *not definitely not* was enough to spark my curiosity.

The following summer I set out to learn what I could about this native predator and see whether I could find one if I was actively looking. I hiked the Wallowas, the Blue Mountains, and the Cascades. I went alone. And along the way I found the most remote places I've ever come across in Oregon.

Random Thoughts from a Month Hiking in Cougar Territory

Of the few people (almost none) I encounter in the deep woods, probably most are carrying weapons. I was told by many friends to bring a gun on this trip. I figured a gun was hugely more dangerous than a cougar, so I've compromised by bringing bear mace.

I have a newfound respect for hunters. What they do is not easy. It takes skill and patience. And many of them seem to have a relationship with the land that is much more profound than what's possible being an environmentalist from your living room in Portland.

It's largely a matter of luck whether a person out here sees a cougar— most of these hunters never will—it being left to each individual to assess whether that luck is good or bad. One skill, though, lies in how we pay attention. Instinctively, we look for things where we can see them. I think of the Buddhist parable of Nasruddin, who was looking for the key to his house under a lamppost. Some friends came upon him and helped him look. Eventually, someone asked where he had lost the key. "Inside," he said. "Then why are you looking for it here?" "There is more light here," he said. I find myself anticipating a cougar right there in the open grass, in the one place where I could easily see him. I must practice looking where the cougar would like to be, not where I could see him, keeping in mind that he is a master of going unseen. So...in that dense foliage there, behind that log, underneath that outcropping, in the shadows...

It's reassuring how close to town you can find real wilds. No one who has spent much time in Forest Park in Portland should be surprised, but it's an nth degree out here.

On trying and not trying to see a mountain lion. I'm here to give myself a chance of seeing a cougar, but I'm scared as hell of actually doing so. I'm deep in the area, though, so if it happens it happens and I'll deal with my emotions later. It keeps me alert, though, to say the least.

This forest has me highly attuned to my status as meat. I could pass ten feet from a cat up here and never see it.

I read somewhere that there are four groups of people most likely to think positively of cougars and other predators: self-identified "wildlife enthusiasts," people with a high socioeconomic status, people who don't own livestock, and young people. I'm 4/4.

There's this superstitious part of me that thinks that if a cougar saw me it would recognize in me what I recognize in it: a common demeanor:

balanced, poised, powerful, self-reliant, graceful—but probably that's the kind of thinking that if I do see a cougar will get me into trouble.

In retrospect, it was probably a bad idea to read so much about cougar attacks before coming out here. As rare as they are, they're now seared into my consciousness. Even though I know what I want to do if I see one (take pictures, then hope for the best), I'd rather have seen one in the past tense than continue to live in the conditional, never mind the present.

The map I got from the forest ranger says, "Oregon. We love dreamers." I must be an Oregonian then.

Compared to my normal hiking, the miles are coming slowly this trip. But the observations come quicker, as I'm more attentive with my attention.

As I take out my tape recorder to make notes rather than having to sit down and take out pen and paper, it's startling to hear my voice even as I whisper and speak about twenty words per minute. I haven't talked to anyone in days.

The longer I go without seeing anything carnivorous the less doing so seems like a real possibility and the less cautious I become—by the ends of these hikes, tired, I'm head-down going for the finish and unless a cougar walks up and says hello, I'm going to miss it.

It would be impossible to overstate a forest's ability to cool the air on a hot day.

Seems important the absence of trail signs. These forests are not the high-use parks and wilderness areas I'm accustomed to. With no maps or signs navigation takes on a whole new level of interest.

Fucking gunfire in the valley below here. It's not yet deer season. Must be target practice. Whether or not the other animals are spooked, I sure am.

Not seeing a cougar this trip I'll be content to imagine at least one has seen me.

Axel Jump

Christine Stewart-Nuñez

I don't know
as I straddle him
on his dining-room chair
that beneath us
the laces on the skates
of his daughter, three years
younger than I,
unravel. On the rink,
I watched his legs cross
and crisscross, unzipping
the iced surface.
Forward, backward—
his footwork serpentine
where the arena
curved. He tugged
off his gloves to write
down my number—
calloused palms, nicked
skin—and I pictured
his hands tuning
transmissions, gripping
tools, steel, me.

He didn't try to ply
me with drinks like
the college guys. Days
of space, a well-placed
compliment were his
offerings. Steadying
me, hands on my bare
shoulders, he holds
my eyes in a hot-iced
gaze. In the hatch pattern
of hazel, I see myself
reverse.

Love Birds

In Izhvesk, a once-closed city, factories anchor
shoreline, churn sludge into a reservoir, blow

plumes of smoke from chimneys like cigarettes
sticking out of concrete blocks. The economy's

core— the AK-47 of Kalashnikov's design,
hunting rifles, pistols—employs everyone.

Near the city square, a monument to industrial
soldiers: a bronze man fitted with boots, pants

wrapping chiseled thighs, arm hoisting
a flag. A wedding party poses: bride's white

cocktail dress against groom's black suit. Camera
clicks, vodka glasses clink. Two birds, fluffy

and white with black neckbands, ignore
the perpetual flame, metal-tinged air, couple's

Love Birds

sweaty sheen of wedding work; their claws
scratch along cement, shuffle toward each other,

feathered breasts touching as they meet.

I Was Thirteen

John Michael Flynn

I looked up. There sat the ghost of Ty Cobb
on a stool in a corner with his *Tigers* uniform on.
He was filing the edges of his steel cleats.
I hurried to one of my prized baseball books,
found a black-and-white photo of Cobb
in mid-air, cleats gleaming, both legs out
like torpedoes as he slid into second base.

I had blood in me. I could do anything.
I rubbed and worked oil into my glove,
limbering up my dreams of baseball summers.
I told Ty Cobb that I had not reached the end.
I'd get somewhere, become somebody.
He just smirked, head down in that corner
rasping steel on steel, his cleats growing sharp.

Abalone

Tobi Cogswell

The perfect pearl
thick with platinum and shined
with dignity and respect.
Smell of wax, cut grass,
and nostalgia
like the days of barber poles,
white gloves and library cards,
beekeepers and family dinners.

A sweet wide seat for sitting close,
radio that plays only blues and bible -
close your eyes at the railroad crossing,
listen for the gate to go up,
you are in a town checkerboarded
with roads and not much else.

You wear white t-shirts,
she wears heels.
You have a flask,
she has lipstick, and the filmiest
scarf - she looks like Sophia Loren
in some movie you can't see

at the drive-in anymore.
You call her *doll*, she blushes.

A windshield wide as a wharf,
thick white sidewalls, and a wish
not everyone has the hunger
to make come true. Fingertips
grazing on that smooth shine
grandly waken a concerto for one.

At Altitude

Jackson, Mississippi

Her skin was the color
of an Indian summer
on the Sunflower River
with light full blazing.

She had two babies, tall
as roadside blossoms,
one in a dress yellow
as field daisies, the other
in the rusted color
of old rail spikes.

She kept them neat and quiet,
but when hungry they could
howl up the dead with a witches
broom of screams.

Her husband had the bottles—
he and his honeysuckle vodka

gone, vanished in an airplane even
skinny folk couldn't hide in.

No one looked at her, mostly
stared at her girls, bright
as summers on the Natchez Trace,
mean-willed as weather.

I took one baby, bounced her
as she played with my glasses.
My man took the other.
Our new woman friend,
beaten with shame and humbled
with anger, patted our shoulders,
went searching for milk.

We knew she'd be back,
kissed each other over the tops
of those sweet babies heads,
wished we could keep them
just a little bit longer, however
long that was gonna be,
just a little bit longer.

Carlos Arredondo Saves His Son

Cindy Hines

My son says you can tell if you're dreaming by looking at a clock.
When you are dreaming, time stands still.
For you, time has stood still for almost a decade
and, yet, you are not dreaming.
You wanted it to be a nightmare you could wake from,
the day the three Marines in dress blues arrived at your home.
They, just representations of your need to defend
your beliefs, your values, and your opinions.
Their blue uniforms signifying your devotion to your son.
If you were lucid, then it was a mistake,
because it is never your own child who dies,
surrounded by the enemy while the sun shines,
shot to death by bullets as rapid as the ticking of a clock.

When you are dreaming, nothing can hurt you
and, if you are in pain, it is a figment of your imagination.
You can smash the windshield of a government van.
You can douse it and yourself with gasoline.
You can light a propane torch and nothing will happen.
Even if it does, the explosion will jolt you awake.
You will be covered in sweat, heart racing, body shaking.
But you can throw off the covers, take a deep breath,

and tell yourself that it is all a dream.
Your son is still a small child, sound asleep in his bed,
Winnie the Pooh tucked under his arm,
his favorite shoes and soccer ball strewn on the floor.
You can kiss his forehead, straighten the covers,
and whisper, "I love you."

But you awake to a body covered in burns,
all the way down to your ticking heart.
At the funeral, you lie on a stretcher,
whispering a vow to your son in his flag-draped coffin.
The sun reflects off every broken piece of glass on the pavement.
The 21-gun salute ricochets off a four-story hotel in Iraq.

The world must remember your son,
and all the sons and daughters who are fighting and dying.
War must end.

In the coming years, you stand on West 43rd Street in Times Square,
shivering in the morning chill.
Your pickup truck, a mobile memorial to your son.
The clock moves, but time stands still for you
until the day that you can save someone's child.

Every year, you hand out flags at the Boston Marathon,
representations of your devotion to your son.
On April 15, 2013, an explosion jolts you awake.
It causes the clocks to run backward, you to travel in time.
You are in Iraq nine years earlier and there is your son.

He is lying wounded amidst shards of glass glistening in the sun.
You run to him, put out the fire on his shirt with your hands,
not feeling the burn, only the ticking of your heart.
You rip your clothes to make a tourniquet for his leg,
carry him in your arms as you did when he was a child,
place him tenderly in a wheelchair,
and run with him to the nearest ambulance.
On this day, you save a son.

Akemi Running

Robert Kostuck

Stumbled exhilaration on the Sandia Crest: the only desire I feel is to go higher, look straight up into a sub-penultimate indigo sphere. Reduced oxygen makes me lightheaded, slightly squeaky-voiced, a bloody tear on my left hand bright red against the first snow—doesn't matter, material world behind and below, basic brown New Mexico an unobtainable rumpled quilt. Akemi spoils it a bit—sprinting a couple hundred yards to the restaurant/gift shop. She'll never stop running. Moments later I catch up—too late: momentarily distracted with her camera she turns and I pick a shred of wet seaweed from her hair, premonition against the day.

Mountain decked in excitable spruce, fir, oak; overcast sky shedding faint snow. Of course I'm reminded of the Canadian Rockies—two hundred kilometers from Edmonton and once I was old enough to have a job and a car, my favored weekend destination. Two years ago feels like forever. Sluiced into my memories: the smell of my mother's filter cigarettes, her hoarse cough, advice that sounds like accusations, uneven guidance about diet and weight gain.

Aloof, Akemi and I walk unhindered, ice swarm, kanji snowflakes, pine whisper; warm air rises, circles Sandia Crest, tightens topside into a foggy spiral chatter galaxy, untended beekeeper, omniscient ornithologist occupation. Two raucous gray mountain birds glorify Akemi's shutter speed, balanced on a thin sandstone reef she records another leg of her escape from Fukuoka, halftone proof sheet of tiny images never published, how she develops reasons for always leaving; Tokyo, Ginza, Paris, Venice, Shanghai, Beijing, Pondicherry—vast resumes of ionized kinetic energy. Albuquerque a quaint train station on her never-gonna-stop journey.

At the top clouds come and go as equals, same altitude, good and bad words flatten out into pure sound. I imagine remembering this tomorrow: returned soon enough to school, home, house, bed where I will iron out the cryptogram she leaves behind, follow a path of wind-scattered kanji candy wrappers, the word *kami* meaning hair, paper, god; a high desert trial open to interpretation, elevated, levitated— "Take this!"—she tosses me her camera, film canisters, quick instructions on developing black and white photographs, lift, vector, arc and inclination, 'borrowed' anima, cartographic insight, ability to interpolate a scattering of surface rocks that may-or-may-not be prehistoric wall remnants, enclosure, encyclopedia of extemporaneous endings; launched lunchtime, sandwiches with flaccid dill sprigs, hard chocolate bars, icy water, caroming carrot sticks; a fine meal, tea ceremony for two. Sets the shutter on automatic, records we two; or, one plus one.

"Now smile."

"Like this?"

"No, sweetie, like this."

A cold hand slides under my jacket and across the small of my back. Of course I scream. When a handful of snow hits the back of her neck Akemi screams, too. Hilarious remember-when moments, through it she triggers the shutter, devised memorandum, evidence in black and white. I secretly add to a photo album with pink covers; pink albums being four dollars less expensive than black or green.

The hike down is quick, jarred teeth, drummed heels. My second-hand Datsun in the dirt parking lot at the base of the trail. It coughs a bit, shudders, *vrooms*; I'll have to look at that. I keep it in order, intricacies of automobile engines: something I learned from my father before he went away.

The rewards come at night: improbable *el norte*-bound javalina root up flower beds, gardens; or a sharp crunch: those wild peccaries eat wormy low-hanging apples right from the tree. Ginger: our dog's in heat and a crazy coyote smells the pheromone of uterine canine blood, defecates on dead grass by the locked front screen door, feces flecked with tiny femurs, dime-sized skulls, fur. Two great horned owls perch on the roof edge, strong hoots rooted just behind the wishbone, rattled down the flue.

Akemi awake on the pounded futon, still as an icicle on a gravel road. Stretches like a spandex housecat. Angles out her elbows, turns her face away, black hair a tangle of forks in the road.

"I couldn't leave here without climbing that mountain at least once."

"I'll make some tea," I say.

Dokudami, some grain concoction that never went near a tea plantation. Her favorite. When I return to the bed she sleep talks, mumbled Japanese I can't understand. The monologue becomes a light snore. Ginger and I sit on the porch steps, her leash tied to the rail. I sip medicinal tea, audibly dare the coyote to return. Across the Pacific Ocean I imagine pre-dawn light in Japan, miso soup for breakfast, commuter trains packed before sunrise proper.

By midnight my elaborate fantasies spin out of control; too many what-ifs? with a healthy dose of what-might-have-beens, quiet stories with occasional pink ululations extracted from talon-raked rabbits who should know better. All bones bend slightly, old skeletons remain long enough for larval songs of decay. What do I know about skeletons? Natural radio plays this song twenty-four hours a day, and behind me, sneaky—

"Jasmine," says Akemi. "Maybe you should see a therapist. Spend less time talking to the air. Spend more time with Miss Asian Bliss: I'll be your everything: salty-sour-bitter-sweet."

"What time is it?" I say.

"Lunchtime in Japan. Come back to bed."

"Fried eggs? Kombu dashi?"

Kombu's in a kitchen counter jar. She microwaves a bowl of water, leaves the leaves to soak for breakfast in a few hours. Patiently awaits.

"Look." I point at the base of the wall. "This plant? These flowers?"

"Very pretty," says Akemi. "Brew."

"*Blue.* Rosemary flowers. A spice? An herb? I'll make pizza for dinner." I crush some between my fingers. She smiles, completely trusted, incompletely understood. Sunrise, I surprise myself. Why am I planning dinner if not to guarantee her safe recovery from a hard bed? I'll be sleepy all day, so—

"You have your soup. I need to sleep."

Rarified desert air in mountain night, tinged with ozone and second-sight, seasoned with sunburned radium, uranium, we glow like meteorites, excite amazing histories, connive against the future. We tangle like salamanders, ferruginous hawks, swordfish: become a chemical delirium, spurn oxygen, ignite. A dream is like being awake; or maybe I'm still awake. Her black hair and very light skin, erotic Kyūshū freckles, sweet fingernails, fingertip artist scars, biting teeth and oh-so-scientific cosmic rays push down on need and want. My short blond hair and awkward investigations. We traverse the spectrum of visible light, articulate the range of radio signals. One minute a wave, next minute a particle. That's something quantum.

Stupid radio pop songs, corny get-well cards, a bouquet of flowers from the convenience store, futon frame cracked in two, sheets speckled with grains of may-be-Japanese bridal rice. Honeymoon like a trial immediately followed with a what-should-we-talk-about-now sentence called friendship. Akemi already snoring, drooling on the pillow. That makes it more possible, more necessary as each night grows shorter. This night of chairs and lust tucks marble feet into a dusty mouth, replenishes my eyes with luminescent fishes and naked blue lizards. This night grows full of teeth, raku, icicles; dead roses that spill, in spite of logic, from gallon jars of crystallized honey. I am filled up with kitchen knives, Etruscan rust, exotic flowers of red on red. Tubes of easel paint melt under the desk lamp. A morning sky ripens, scours away those flame red clouds on the horizon. Nothing will ever stand still again

One wakes and plans a lunch menu. One eats dinner with one's eyes: boiled foil pouches, Indonesian soda-pop flavored hard candy, tablespoon chunks of 'Indian' curry, instant mashed potatoes, mint-chocolate chip ice cream, katsuobushi curling above sticky rice, daikon minced to atoms, frozen peas and carrots, canned adzuki beans, umeboshi paste. I gain weight just inhaling the steam, push away my bowl. Eating with chopsticks I lose track of the servings.

One wakes and drinks French roast, Columbian, Vienna blend. It's just possible. She works at a frame shop Monday to Friday: I work off and on, here and there. Right now it's off and here. Sunday is our domestic day.

One spies on Akemi slipping out the door, narrow shoes, nylon track suit, mittens; already thin as a shadow.

"Borderline anorexic. You need potassium or complex carbs or fruit maybe? Bananas, figs? Oatmeal?"

She laughs at that, launches into the five-mile morning.

"This inexcusable cornucopia," I say to Ginger. "You know? Just. Way. Too. Much. Your coyote boyfriend has the right idea: eat the mouse, vole, wood rat, house cat. Eat everything and shit out the bones." Ginger attentive and not caring. It's a dog's life.

Wind shushes through dark trees, oil paint smells so good, prelude to each day's dreams

comprised of colors, awkward written words, dirty dishes. Winter and summer blend in this recitation, cold and white, warm and green, a red and brown bird perched very still on a gray line of numbers, calendar montage dropped on the crackle hearth of burned wood, her arm around my shoulder, drip of melted snow (already?), tense flap of geese and ducks; it drags me down to the place of borders and edges. I collect seed pods in the alleys and execute sketchy seed pod realism, arbitrate the existence of genetics: XX/XY gets lost in the night, précis of our XX/XX concavity, me, alone, faint watercolors crafted from broken possibilities, organic jewelry inspirations, brown ova still-life neatly arrayed on my worktable.

That afternoon: a brief heavy rain; unexpected, out of place in October, washes away crinkle-cut leaves, tamps dust, muddies the Rio Grande. Akemi cursing in the darkroom, weather, humidity, problematic liquids, gray scales, mountain birds. Landscapes, still lifes, fabrics and textures, nude models. She frequently photographs herself naked—the long wire that trips the shutter—works darkroom shadow and light magic, makes herself look thinner, invisible, and there's something wrong about that disappearing act. Photographs me naked, artistic sprawl, embarrassed flabby non-centerfold. I cringe at photos of myself exposed and unhealthy, plain and ugly. She insists: every woman is beautiful. What would mother say?

My workbench and clip-on desk lamp, pliers and thin awls, tin snips and files, slivers of silver and copper, gleaming semi-precious stones, crinkle of turquoise, opaque jade poise, jaded bloody garnet glow; I reach for the proper tool, fasten logarithm ligaments around handles, hafts, heft the dull sheen of lead; reversible drill, hatchet, and saws: crosscut-, miter-, saber-, keyhole-, rip-, hack-; chisels, rasps, hones.

"It was here a minute ago—things keep disappearing." Look over and past Akemi's left shoulder. "Screwdriver I sharpened down for a chisel. Missing in action, it was right here."

"Do I look like—?"

"Number one suspect."

"This is getting stupid."

"It was right here."

Akemi shoves aside newspapers, ashtray, loose tobacco, broken pencils.

"You mean this?"

"Dang, second pair of eyes. I apologize."

Her easel and paintbrushes, acrylic tubes, oil pastels, canvas, paper, sketchbooks, colored pencils; annex of darkroom and chemistry, light and dark, trickle of water, toxic sink, sticky photography paper and I'm already out the door, dirt yard, autumn, self-eradicating hejira.

Sit on a weathered kitchen chair, roll a cigarette. Full morning sun, the adobe wall Navajo white, white chocolate white, chalk, cream, taupe, tannic acid yellow, chrome yellow, sand yellow, silt ocher, mustard sienna, acrid umber; pointillist vectors of Manzanita red, goblin blue, Paris green, Royal purple, French gray, ebon…. Smoke congeals in the still air, a slushy sound that might be automobiles on the other side of the fence. I'm sort of alone.

"Mother," I say, "I see you there behind that sycamore tree—see your coat—if you want to play hide-and-seek, fine. I never gave a shit. What? Speak your lines? I could. I could use a funny voice to keep our words separate."

"Jasmine you need to stick to that diet. Make your body a prize or a weapon," says Mother-from-my-mouth.

"I'm at the bottom of the ocean," I say.

"Why sweetie are you drowning?"

"No mother I'm living in the United States. Drowning is a metaphor for sensory overload, and yes, too much food. Must you?"

"You were the one wanted to leave."

"I'm not complaining."

"Of course Roy and I have moved—his transfer—we live in Vancouver now—so there's nowhere in Edmonton for you to come back to—"

"I'm happy here in New Mexico."

"Fighting with your Chinese roommate—girlfriend—lover—?"

"She's Japanese and the best friend I've ever had."

"You'll outgrow this infatuation. Some art student thing, a phase—"

"You've never experienced—"

"You accused her—"

"I refuse to argue with you."

"Who are you talking to?" Akemi framed, door held open, expensive warm air pouring into the chilly day.

"You heating the outdoors?" I say.

"You worry too much about money," says Akemi.

"Excuse me, I need to make a private phone call."

But my mother's number is no longer in service.

Rainwater sliding down the window, satisfactory strips of shingle the landlord nailed over last summer's slow roof leaks. I'll go out into the oxidized world of brown, gray, burnt orange; faint raven iridescence, pale blue wood smoke, zinc and silver chain-link fences. Scruffy October, a lack of fresh snow, a harvest basket of bright pastoral quintessential reds, blues, and yellows lingering on the bellies and backs of winter birds. She's a camera, I'm a fat ghost story. Our home life reduced to Spartan cells, but we give each other haircuts in the kitchen. Every day I walk WPA sidewalks toward endlessly branching desert jeep trails, summer nights, relentless heat, bundled clouds and heat lightning, a three quarter moon. New road signs go up: Proceed With Caution, No U-Turn, Yield. Newspaper headline predictions: Día de los Muertos, La Posada, Happy New Year. My heart says: none of this is true.

One Friday morning she goes running, refuses to return for two days. Sunday afternoon, warm day already starting to cool, outside on that old chair I smoke a Fibonacci series of cigarettes, pick up a coffee cup and set it down without drinking any. Akemi smells of ocean, leans in for a kiss, spills sand from sleeves and hair. My hand shakes and the cigarette smoke makes zigzag lines in the air. I fake not caring.

"Guess I'll go shower."

"Wash off that sea foam," I say.

"Sea foam," she says, her face a series of photographs: stout fish with push-pin teeth and poison spine tips, loose seaweed coating the water's surface like oil, broken iridescent seashells that might be mermaid earrings, reefs visible at low tide that might be sunken ships, a place where sky meets sea that might be a goal-like horizon.

"That's Japan."

"Well, yes. Where else?" she says.

While she showers away vacation postcards I pour the coffee on the ground, bang kitchen cupboards for eradication. All I find is a half-dozen swallows of tequila and the first gulp burns. I change into an extra large t-shirt I wear instead of pajamas. She exits the bathroom and my glass is half full. Peels away damp towels, naked, brown, sexy runner legs, probably pissed off, already getting dressed and packing a camera bag with many side pockets.

"Gee I hate to be a bitch—" she says.

"Are you leaving again?" I sound like my mother, clingy, worried about being left alone; alone being her worst companion. She had her cigarettes, I've got cigarettes and half a glass of tequila.

"I'm going down by the river to photograph the water. If you must know. It's the light, this gray light—"

I stand in the doorway. She leans from my car window.

"You heating the outdoors?" she says. "You worry too much about everything. Go put on some pants before you freeze to death."

Inside, kitchen table, my mother and her daughter. We push a cellophane package of cigarettes back and forth. Practical looks verge on I-told-you-so.

"You're a pretty girl and I guess by now you know something about seduction," she says. "Lose a few pounds, work on that complexion, a little makeup, and you'll be a perfect ten. Maybe one of those medical students. Clean-cut, easily manipulated, and sweetie once he's hooked—once you've got that ring on your finger—you've got a place to fight from."

"Does it have to be a fight?" I say. "And why can't it be another woman, another artist? Akemi's—"

"—she's already gone. You know that." Mother mashes out her cigarette, takes my hand. "It's about survival. Where are you going to be in twenty-five years? Imagine being fifty. Personally I don't give two shakes of a rat's tail if you're with another woman. The point is, she's leaving. Already gone. What happens next? And that rescue mutt you took in. Tawny—Amber—"

"Her name's Ginger and we both adopted her."

"You adopted her and your partner went along with it. You thought if you had a baby your girlfriend would stay. But you're the only one takes care of the dog. Sweetie some people just don't give a damn, pardon my language. Babies, dogs, spoken commitments—a marriage license is a business contract, it offers options and security— something to at least think about—"

"Mother, I think—" but she's gone. I call her friend Mavis in Edmonton and leave a message, empty the glass, wrap my arms around a pink photo album, sleep the sleep of the just. Wake to the light of dusk or dawn with a dry mouth and Akemi yanking off layers of cotton and wool, kicking shoes across the room.

"Half drunk?" she says. "Easier to take advantage." Her laugh is exactly halfway between goofy and wicked.

Curls next to me, grabs my shoulders, glides harsh palms across my overweight body, bulging stomach, thick thighs, wobbly breasts. Akemi spills tiny seashells and delicate seabird feathers; she smells of calm tidal pools and tastes like vanilla salt water taffy.

In our kitchen someone flicks a cheap cigarette lighter, coughs.

Halloween. She takes off running and does not come back for five days. I leave on the porch light, hand out crappy candy to fairies and superheroes, cartoon characters I do not recognize. Eat what's left of the junk food and start in on a new bottle of Blue Agave tequila with some spiky Mexican cactus on the label. She's in the door before I notice I'm not alone. Stands in front of me. Evaluates. Fancy athletic shoes, tight leggings, fleece jacket; fishy sweat odor and she's almost hyperventilating. No seaweed, sand, or seashells; only the sound of ocean waves on a pristine Japanese beach. I feel pretty and high; spiky, frisky.

"Back so soon?" I say.

"It's called exercise. You should try it sometime." Grabs my glass, takes a sip.

"Now you're showing off. So healthy you can afford to indulge."

"You're showing off too. How self-indulgent and depressed you can be."

"And how bulimic you can be," I say. "I'm not stupid. You run to the bathroom and you're throwing up! I hear you! Your big secret. You brush your teeth fifty times a day. And let me tell you. At least I'm not a puking fashion model wanna-be."

She slams the bedroom door. I lean over the toilet and vomit up chocolate and alcohol; fall asleep sitting at the kitchen table. Mother touches my hand. We sit there like that all night. I'm alone again, paging through my half-empty pink loves-me-loves-me-not photo album.

I watch Akemi and two women I don't know pack boxes, fill the bed of a pickup truck. Two weeks pass, a month, December before you know it. The reek of photographic chemicals lingers. There's no address, just a cell number. She leaves me stripped bare by imagined multiple brides, creative acts reduced to maudlin repetition, slim diary of what I've learned: mostly anecdotes involving the loss of imagination. Leaves me with a need to fill the emptiness of her dark room, a need to fill the tempered space where I pretend tangible loss is a storage compartment for my own wordless staying-in-place.

I write to mother in Vancouver and tell her about my rapid weight loss, my devoted rescue dog Ginger, my three point zero grade point average, my part-time job as a model in the drawing classes, my part-time job at a local fender shop where the men treat me like one of the guys. How I lie to complete strangers about dating three different fellows—medical students in their fourth year—when really I hang out at Nines, the local lesbian bar n' grill. Tell her how I jog in a gray sweat suit, prepare healthy meals of vegetables and grain, throw up when I've had too much to eat or drink; or anytime I feel fat, ugly, or stupid. Photographs of me will show a mathematical line with no dimensions. Soon I'll be wafer thin, fashion model beautiful, vanquished, vanished, invisible. I'll call it survival. Mother will understand and approve.

Book of Lights

Jeff Fearnside

We all derive from the same source. There is no mystery about the origin of things. We are all part of creation, all kings, all poets, all musicians; we have only to open up, only to discover what is already there.

—Henry Miller

listen:there's a hell
of a good universe next door;let's go.

—e.e. cummings

I

In the painting by Cossiers
he looks like an animal:
scrunched up and hairy, wild-eyed,
legs like scrub oak, twisted and bunched,
and in his hands a thick stalk of fennel, a hollow wrapper
bulging with the sweet candy it contains:
fire.

(You're reaching, see, but you can only see
as high as the top shelf,

and the clean trail through the dust there,
and the label rubbed raw from repeated caresses.)

Fire in the hold! There's a fire
in the belly of the ship
with the dragon-headed prow
moving its thick, slow hull,
a husk through the water
(all right, it's in a bottle, and your quivering
fingers are having a hard time tying the rigging).

You should have been a set of fiery scales
flying through the earth's fiery gut.

Instead you slay old symbols
and with them their home:
　　driving mine shafts deeper,
　　testing bomb drops deeper,
　　dropping glowing waste in concrete and hoping
it won't leak into our aquifers
or detour us from the prophets
under the soil: mineral signposts to rivers of oil
and roads of lead, zinc, copper, silver and gold,
tailings from which you leave like a trail
of stale crumbs to find your way home
until the hole is empty.

Your life is a mirror of itself,
an infinitely reflecting set of nested cups,

each a harbor where ships drown themselves.
I see England, I see France, I see Pandora's underpants!
"If she ain't good enough for that ol' boy with fire, I don't want her;
so what of her dowry?"

The land of Inspector Clouseau will burn
its collective toes if it's not careful where it drops its tests.
Those who grew up in the fifties' American West
better hope they didn't drink the milk downwind of Nevada.
The Bikini Atoll isn't shaking her hips so good after all these years,
      either;
better give her a mammogram.

II

Lady Madonna, spirit at your feet,
where'd you get the body to hold that sheet?

"If Jesus was the son of man
then you've known the whole world,
and for my part I must say
I've enjoyed our little tryst, my *virgencita*."

Is that a sword clutched in those tiny
hands wrapped in aura and straw?

III

At dusk, lights shining brightly
inside send brick walls thrusting

outside, painted in reflection
violet blue and sunset blood.

You feel as if you could walk
down the mirrored hallway, suspended
in air, no longer solid,
lit from within by a sub-atomic light
switch being rapidly flicked on and off.

Your mental body casts
shadows in this staccato light—
like the flickering ghost of old Oppenheimer,
giddy with the notion of the invisible
fingers on the hands of his electrons
holding up the world;
like the shadows in the corridor
when the train rolls by your window;
like the shifting of gears in the car by the stoplight,
the shifting of shadowed red in movement on that Mustang
as the cycle of lights completes its circuit:
the blink of the crosswalk sign from white *walk*
to winking *don't walk,*
the shift of phase from green to yellow
on the horizontal slice of street (anticipation of the gears,
then), from red to green on the intersected paved plane.

Only a man's trunk is seen, the rest
swallowed by the equestrian vehicle
supporting him from beneath.

Is that you Pyrrha,
standing there in traffic?

Just think of a wheel stopped,
the face of a clock in a dusty attic, unused
and broken, left in a box with rusty ball bearings
and newspapers colored with age. The harvest
moon is out tonight, full and yellow, hanging
like a paper lantern over the river,
its light singing low,
the notes bending from the weight of smog.

There's your true north.

IV
Walking behind a goddess—every step,
planned and sure, makes her calves
quiver, flesh firm to the bone,
an electric shape clinging to fabric
and outlining itself round. You are reminded
of a nighttime stroll on the beach,
the delightful arc of her feet from beach to air
and back to beach again, kicking up sand,
sending curling lines of amber glass into the surf.

From behind you saw her half-turn,
and her exposed eye looked to you, a wide
circle of brown, before she fell
into the alluvial mud.

The great flood will come, her father-
in-law had warned, but he didn't say
what form the resurrection would take.

V

The old oak pyre is smoking
in a forked tier of light,
split tongues twining a braid
of flame about a bloated pig,
squeezing out its life and locking
in its fuel and juices,
tender victuals flowing for the hypostasis.

The bones are bundled in tripe and fat,
the select morsels stuffed in an unappealing sausage hide.
Zeus reaches down his finger (that finger
which directs the jarring traffic of lightning) and points
to the larger pile of charred bone plumped by its glistening cloak;
the sack of good meat he leaves,
and by his oath must live by his choice.
The old boy foiled him! That cagey Titan
fooled the Father—and was paid with the beak of a bird
pecking at his immortal liver.

Despite his name, he never had the forethought
to pick the locks like Jesus did: Want out? Give up the ghost
and fly away, and in three days come back again.
Neat trick, that, slithering out from underneath the body.
Harry Houdini was even better; he did it while still

alive. Then his soul took a vacation
and checked his bones into a box. *Hello, AT&T.*
A collect call from where? Wait a minute,
the phone's for you.

"Yes, David Copperfield made the Statue of Liberty
disappear, but it must be a trick. What's the trick?
What's the trick? There's no trick?
You picked *what*?"

VI

Body body burning bright...
Make a jungle noise,
something from the belly, from the base
of the skull, yeah,
something drawn-out,
    YEA-AH.
Forget about gazing into that celestial night,
stare point-blank into damnable rock.

[Scene: On an island somewhere
where the top half of the world meets
the bottom on a fecund latitude.]

The great cone shadows the heat within.
Climb into the womb underneath that
giant breast spilling magma at the nipple.
Stab brightly through the smoky
dream of flora ahead—thoughts will kill

you here. Only movement saves. Burmese tygers are
the least of your worries. Better clear your mind—
soft, yellow poppy dreams

> (school busses and speed limits,
>
> rain jackets to keep out the acid
>
> rain, journalistic rags soaked in tinted news,
>
> the jaundiced views of everyone, it seems)

have supplanted your skull's real base
desires—move away from the low
lands, through the valley of the shadow
of riches and pain, and into the fire-misted well.

The mountain is a drop of rock dipped
into the moving pool of the earth's loam.
Dusky hoof prints are scattered on that
uppercutting crust: Follow them,
into the bulging vein of the earth, an inverse
hollow for heaven. Lash at the insides
of the space you're inside,
knees and hands scuffing the floor—
a defiant supplicant's pose.

Scream your delirious, trembling prayer
of affirmation to the figure beside you,
a sound of palm fronds and gastric acid.

Night scrapes low like an artist's bow;
the audience is separated from the stage by the curtain.
Only the players know its workings, *deus ex machina*:

the machine in the ghost of the mountain
that will pluck you like the opposite of dusk
from the currency of blackness you must accept,
for it's all on your account.

Prometheus was nailed to a cliff.
He's bound to you in payment.

VII

Below you, the sheen of street lights and mercury
vapor lamps, neon and headlights,
the flickering blue of television screens
and searchlights on billboards and buildings;
above you, the haze of the city
even outperforming heaven's glow.

Behind you, a shadow crawling into the constellations,
leaving behind his pain in a pile next to yours.

VIII

The bear's heart beats strong in her sleeping blubber,
as the short nights grow longer
into one another. The chill of December
is no greater than the chill in your bones,
so throw your head to the wind and march
to the tone that flows through the marrow—
the dripping of water falling from eaves,
freezing before it gets halfway to ground,

to be held until Springtime
then sent on its cycle home.

Now that the lord of the Centaurs is dead
he aims his long bow at Callisto,
poor animal, chained to Polaris,
never again allowed to bathe
in the world's waters.
Instead, an interminable spiralling chase
to the top of the evening sky.

Beneath the grey on sky is blue.
Beneath enamel the raw nerve waits to be exposed,
to bristle with the shock-breath come
whistling through the rows of nerves, grey
picket fences transmitting a painful,
sweet aching, *that the body of light come forth*
from the body of fire.

Eat your peas and cantos.

It is near like skin.
When the outer layer of its
space lies shed on the floor
of a cool, dark place, it remains—distilled,
like rain water in a barrel
when the barrel has rotted to gravity,
a space of water shimmering, held
in the shape of a barrel. It ebbs

and flows, the space of water moving
to form new shapes:

a baby howling to fill his dark-full belly...
a street light howling, *It is me! It is me!*...
a sparrow flying north late in December...
a low, warbled chord sung by three people...
a thrashing of sweat and white knuckles in bed—

IX

We are an expression of the earth,
Alan Watts believed:

> Flowers flower,
>
> apple trees apple,
>
> oak trees acorn,
>
> the earth peoples.

The world peopled when a tiny figure was hidden from a pedophile
      father,
seen through the clouds then pulled from his substance;
out of spite, more were made.
We are dust mixed with the brackish water of angry tears.

Phaenon, which is your true home,
the cloud-caged heavens above,
or the mud dripping from and of your feet?

Ashes to ashes,
your bloated liver to fields of bitter grain.

X

Madame Sesostris, by way of Eliot
by way of Huxley, by way of Egypt
—peer into her house of cards,
ask her for a reading:

Ah, how fortunate your suffering,
she says, flipping up two cards,
both of the Major Arcana.

Here you see the hierophant,
king of those animals housed in half-human flesh.
He represents your past, his broad human shoulders
squeezing up from the husk of muscle and fur
below like larvae squirming to be born
into butterflies. He is Chiron, whose home you visited.
You have been wounded by the blood of a monster.
You have given it away—the pain was so intense—
do you know to whom?

And here is the scaly future as shown through
the length of Ouroboros, always joined yet always
growing, a static feast.
You can connect your head
to your body only by devouring yourself.
Can't have one without the other,
your mother used to say.
Can't have your chocolate cake
until you eat your Lima beans.

The frosting is on fire, and that bowl
is shaped a lot like a famous bride's box.

But there is one more card, she says, which I have left
out of order. Why? The two on either side
form a cross. Chiron is one arm
of the X, the serpent the other;
the point which they dissect is eternity,
where you struggle to wake from sleep.

The Madame, that seer savant, turns the final card,
which she places in-between the others.

"The Hanged Man—yes, that's him, spread-eagle
(if you'll forgive the pun) upside-down on that boulder.
Some *paté, Monsieur* Our Nation's Symbol?…
Sorry, ma'am, but he sold me a gift
and rotted my gut out, too. Didn't know how to use it right,
he said… What about the book?…
*The kingdom of God is spread upon the earth
and men do not see it.* Do you? Well, you being a woman and all,
I thought… Yes, enough talk."

XI

The son of Iapetus was chained to the soil, the price
of balance: another spirit was staked to a tree,
ransoms paid both for each.
Each of us must prick
our own wrists and watch

the flowers foam and bubble
then slink to the earth.

Prometheus hung for thirty years,
Jesus for two thousand;
Houdini knew the trick, though he forgot it.
If you're good, you might hang around for a day,
or none.

Where We Are Now

Chris Anderson

There is a plaza where you are now
made of stone, and the sun is beating down on it.
The pilgrims are crawling on their hands and knees
to ask Our Lady to help them.

Here there is a forest and the shadows of a forest.
It is afternoon, and Pip and I are climbing
to the top of the hill, where we can look out
over the broad, summer valley.

Tonight, when the candles are burning
and the guitar is playing and you are chanting
with the monks in the dark,
I will be clearing away my dinner things

and washing up the dishes, here in our kitchen,
in our bright, empty house.
Oh my dearest friend, this is the gift I give you
after all these years. I give you my loneliness.

The Dream of the Fisherman's Son

Bruce Douglas Reeves

Stretching on tiptoe, I peered over the crusted black rim of the heavy, sizzling, black skillet at the three bug-eyed, whiskered, twitching catfish. Were they straining to leap out of that bubbling bacon fat? My father, a tall, bulky presence suddenly behind me, dug his thick fingers into my bony five year-old shoulder. The cooking fish smelled and he smelled. Their smells collided. Strong. Not bad. Insistent.

"Don't worry, Petesy—they don't feel a thing."

Liar.

I *saw* them writhing in the smoking cast-iron pan, tails flipping up, heads spastic, eyes huge. They *must've* been in agony as they thrashed their flat tails in the bath of popping fat and grimaced with those pale slashes of mouths. I almost could feel their pain. And when they lay heaped, crisp and glossy, on my mother's pink and white flower-patterned dish, I stared with horror at a greasy pile of fried friends. Was it those stiff whiskers framing the wide, frowning mouth that made me attribute intelligence and sensitivity to the catfish, forgetting that my dad already had gutted—although not beheaded—them before my mother dropped them into the snapping, crackling fat?

He whacked me on the back with his big hand, believing that he was consoling me, but he couldn't understand my revulsion. For him it was simple: he caught the catfish and my mom cooked 'em, so by god I was gonna eat 'em. To refuse was to betray him, to rebel against his position in the family, to deny his manhood. I didn't understand all that then, but I knew that I had no choice.

The agony of those dinners endures. My fingers fumble with the slippery bones and my tongue tries to escape the powerful catfish taste, and I suffer again with the knowledge that sooner or later I'm going to gag on the gray flesh.

I wish that we could've learned to understand each other, to exist in each other's shoes, but his mud-caked work shoes and fishing boots were too big for me. He always gazed over my head, talking at me, but never to me. And yet I never doubted that he loved me.

Evening after silent evening, he bent over our kitchen table, tin boxes scattered like miniature treasure chests across the blotchy landscape of flowered oilcloth, creating small wonders to tempt the wily trout. He wedged a naked hook into the rough black jaw of a steel vise clamped to the side of the table; then, with a flicker of feather, a twist of colored thread, a dot of glitter, a new counterfeit fly came to life.

Hovering behind the wide, stained shoulder of my father's tee shirt, I watched the delicate motions of his dark-nailed hands as he wrapped bright thread around feather fragments and tied luxurious, complicated knots.

"Petesy," he asked, his thick blue-veined arm gathering me into the quivering yellow pool beneath the fringed lamp shade. "If I use this green thread instead of the royal purple, d'you think the fish'll go for it?"

Ignorant and shy, intimidated by his smelly adult male force, I shrugged, silently watching him create a variation on a much-used, time-proven deception.

His many-compartmented tin boxes seemed to buzz with hundreds of flies of every imaginable color and form, yet—an artist never satisfied with his labors—he continued inventing, tying, perfecting. Sometimes, he sold his homemade flies to other fishermen, but more often he gave them away—to friends, to folks he met on the streams. The act of creation was what mattered, second only to the fishing itself.

"Beautiful," said my mom, glancing from the sink where she was washing dishes, but I knew even then that she wasn't really looking. That was just her way, making the noises that she thought her husband wanted to hear. Sometimes, she did the same thing with me when I tried to show her a drawing.

She knew, though, that Sylvester was proud of his skill as a fisherman and needed me to be as passionate about it as he was. Nothing would've made him happier than seeing me, his only son, an expert angler. He pursued any freshwater fish, from lowly catfish to mighty steelhead, but he loved best going after trout—rainbows, German browns, the aristocrats of game fish—and although sometimes he condescended to fish with bait, he never pretended that it compared with the art of fly fishing.

I may have been fascinated by the tying of feathers and thread on those barbed hooks, but that didn't mean I wanted to kill fish. Or eat them.

When I was older, laboring at homework on the opposite end of the table (same table, different town), sometimes I eluded long division by stealing glances across the fading flowers of the oilcloth as the creatures of my father's imagination materialized knot by nimble knot on the barbed hook gripped by the black vise. Numbers danced through my brain with feathery bits of imitation insect, confounding all possibility of accurate calculation.

"Back to work!" scolded mom, who wanted me to make something of myself.

She tolerated being a fishing widow because she had no ambitions for herself or her husband beyond survival and a bit of comfort. Her dreams were reserved for my future. She didn't have a specific career in mind for me, but one that shimmered in blurry magnificence like a scene from a Hollywood musical, and homework would propel me over the first of those Technicolor steps up which I would dance, top hat in hand, to paradise.

I'll build a Stairway to Paradise,
With a new Step ev'ry day.
I'm going to get there at any price;
Stand aside, I'm on my way!

I did my best to concentrate on the rows of numbers, but what textbook could rival the small wisps of peacock feather and pheasant plume that some misty morning would flutter at the end of an invisible line above a plum-colored river? This was magic, and my dad, despite his stained and smelly tee shirt, despite his big, scarred hands and rough voice, was the magician.

Although their beauty enticed me, I never was allowed to play with the bits of feathers or rabbit and skunk fur that my father collected for his sorcery. Mom feared I'd snag a finger on a barbed hook, but his concern was more important: that I'd mutilate his carefully and expensively amassed fly makings. Even if my childish, caressing hands didn't rip apart the fragile bits of feather or the delicate animal hairs, the oils from the tips of my fingers would smudge their shimmering colors, destroying their lightness and perfection.

Sylvester escaped the punishing routine of his job and the boredom of family responsibilities with what he called "the sport of kings," and his goal was to turn me into a replica of himself: a junior-sized master angler.

"I was just a kid," he told me, "when I learned to fish. It saved my life later. During the Depression, hunting and fishing helped keep me from starving."

I came to admire his skill on the stream as well as tying flies, but I wasn't him and never could be. His orations flew around me like shrapnel, occasionally striking, but more often whizzing past my young body.

Sporting magazines gaudy with leaping German browns and rainbow trout arching in midair over variegated pools were scattered across tables and chairs, their color covers tacked and taped to the walls of our rented houses. Rods and creels and many-pocketed vests littered the small, crowded rooms, yet those objects held no romance for me.

Despite my fascination with the fake flies, I grew into a matter-of-fact kid, more involved with my own primitive existence than with gentlemanly adventures on field and stream. I refused to be impressed by the dog-eared snapshots of the triumphant angler flaunting his catch that were tacked over dressers, beds, and kitchen counters. I was beginning to have my own dreams, my own ambitions.

Sylvester was always trying to get me outside, trudging along the stream with him, even if I didn't hold a pole, at least searching for wild asparagus or spotting the fish in the deep pools or birds in trees and bushes.

"You can't read and draw pictures all the time. You've gotta learn to be one of the boys, to fit in."

In other words, be an athlete, a sportsman, a hunter, a fisherman.

I groaned, but knew better than to protest. Fortunately, most of the time he didn't want to bother with a kid tagging along when he went off to do serious fishing.

However, even I came near to being awed the year I was eight, when a photo of my parents appeared in the center of the Sunday sports page among shots of opening day anglers. A *Tribune* staff photographer caught my parents on the sloping shore above a mountain dam, posing them on either side of a rod weighted down with ten rigid trout suspended from grotesquely stretched mouths. The joke, which didn't escape me even then, was that this was the only time in memory that mom let my dad persuade her to go out with him on one of those early morning expeditions and to even hold a rod in her pale, housewife's hands.

"Look at her!" he crowed, pointing to the black and white photo. "A real fisher gal!"

And he slapped her affectionately on the fanny.

"Sylvester!" she protested, but her blue eyes sparkled with pleasure. Just the same, though, I don't think he ever got her out with a pole in her hands again.

Dad's first serious attempt to initiate me into his passion came a year later, after we moved to Idaho, near some of the world's best trout streams. Before this, I'd only tagged along with my parents (Louise brooding in the car as she paged through *Modern Screen* and *Photoplay* while Sylvester stalked the ghostly tenants of the stream), occasionally holding a pole and pulling out a minnow or two, but now just the two of us, dad and I, were venturing on an all-day fishing expedition.

Two sports leading the sporting life.

I'm sure that the idea of the outing seduced him more than anything else. He pictured himself as a model *Boy's Life* father, a Norman Rockwell picture of a dad, launching his nine year-old son into the rituals of manhood. Although neither imposing as an individual nor powerful in his life, he could do this for me. So he marched me along the half-tame mountain river, demonstrating casting and strategy, and whispering with melodramatic reverence in which gloomy pools the big ones lurked. There was always a Granddaddy Fish that perversely eluded all but the most crafty fisherman. I imagined this fat, wise old fish watching us with bulbous eyes through the cloudy water, snickering to himself as we dangled obviously fake lures over his blunt nose.

By mid-afternoon (this was summer and the days were long and we'd been up since dawn), my feet were stumbling over the pebbled river banks and my muscles were weary from the deliberate pace my father demanded. That year, I'd discovered the thrills of science fiction and longed to slip off to the lumpy back seat of our old Plymouth to hunker down with the saga of intergalactic warfare I'd smuggled along. At nine years old, I wanted to conquer the universe not a damn fish. I didn't need to prove that I was a man. I didn't want to prove anything, except that I was master of the solar system.

"Dad," I began several times, aiming my words at the back of his old plaid shirt. "Dad, do you think that I...."

Each time that I started to ask if I could hike back to the car, the words tangled on my tongue. I was afraid of his temper and, in some half-aware way, of hurting him. So I trudged at his side, tolerating it when he showed me off to old timers we met along the stream (declaring that I was gonna be as good a fisherman as he was before he finished with me).

Of course, nobody asked what I wanted to do. Just as I'd learned from tales of shifty, malicious aliens that the universe was unfathomable, unpredictable, and probably deadly, I'd come to realize that the whims and demands of parents and all other adults were just as dangerous.

You don't know who you're dealing with, I mentally shouted at him, *but someday you will. Wait and see.* Meanwhile, I was at his disposal, obliged to play a part, whether I wanted to or not.

I did my best to cast the line with the same beguiling arc that he launched so effortlessly and to reel it in with the fly hovering weightlessly above the glossy skin of the river, but although I craved dad's approval and tried hard to earn it, my fly jiggled lifelessly through the olive-green water. (*Haw-haw*, laughed the Granddaddy Fish deep under his sheltering river bank.) However, my usually impatient father was surprisingly easy-going that day.

"Those trout down there are sharp," he assured me. "Don't underestimate 'em, but sooner or later one of 'em is gonna grab that fly, son. And then will you have fun!"

I couldn't wait.

After several hours, as if in response to his faith, the slack waggle of my line jerked tight and the almost invisible tip of my slender rod strained toward the water. My father shouted and seemed to grow larger as he swayed next to me between two boulders on the river bank.

"*Hook* him!" his gravelly voice commanded. "Don't let the bastard get away."

Staring with terror at the straining arch of pole and line, I tugged on the rod. A Martian might've been trying to drag me into the poisonous, mucus-like waters of a canal on his native planet.

"*Play* him, boy. Take it easy—he's a good one!"

Knees locked on trembling legs, wrists aching from the weight dragging at my puny arms, I held firm against the vibrating line. This was the first real fish I'd hooked, so I had no way of knowing if what I was experiencing was normal, but my father's excitement alarmed me. The more he shouted, the more confused, the more terrified, I became.

From another, hostile galaxy, I heard a rough, piercing voice commanding me:

"*Damn it, reel in!*"

"Here, give it to me!" he barked. "Give me the goddam pole."

He crashed over the wide, submerged rocks at the river's edge, water blackening his gray trousers up to his thighs, fingers reaching for the jerking rod.

"Leave the boy alone!" scolded one of the old men watching. "Let him bring it in!"

The other old-timers agreed. "That's the *boy's* fish!" shouted another of them. "Let him have it, for Chrisake!"

Reluctantly, my father dragged his rough hand back from the pole. Sheepishly, he peered at the audience scattered on the river bank. Okay, the joy of the catch would be mine, but the excitement of the moment, the thrill of hooking such a big bastard of a fish, erased any frustration he felt. Well, almost. And I knew that I'd better not screw up.

"Keep it *taut*," he prompted, trying like hell to be a good sport. "Slow and steady. Bring him in, Petesy. You can do it."

Of course, he knew I'd flub it, but I concentrated on doing what I thought he wanted me to do. Suddenly, the fish broke the water, a silver bow of straining muscles arching over an explosion of lacy white foam.

"Is *that* the fish?" I blurted. "*That's* what I've got on here?"

"Son of a bitch!" coughed an old man behind me. "That boy's got hisself a *fish!*"

The tendons in my arms burned and the bones in my wrists felt as if they were going to snap, but I was hauling that angry, leaping fish closer to the shore. Dazzling in his life struggle, he glittered like a bunch of silver dollars, splashed with patches of green and pink. But what was I gonna *do* with him—how long would this battle last?

"I've got the net," dad shouted, his stocky sweat-and-river-stained body poised to scoop up my prize. "Bring him over *here*, son, so I can get him in the net!"

His words hung in the scorching sunlight for a minute before I understood their meaning, then I tried to swing the arching rod around, dragging the massive, resisting weight of the fish through the foamy water toward the slick reddish slope of the bank.

"*Here*, son! Over *here*!"

Dad waded into the bottle-green water, then dipped the net under the splashing trout, bringing it up triumphantly, the fish a thrashing, shimmering weight in the webbing.

"Shit!" hollered one of the old-timers. "That must be ten pounds of rainbow you've got there, boy!"

"Feels like fifty!" I groaned.

The old guys guffawed with lusty adult humor and for a moment I felt smug and grown up. I didn't complain when dad carried the net up onto the bank and lifted the fish out of its soggy webbing, as if *he'd* caught it. I even felt proud when he held it high between us, his blunt finger hooked under its saw tooth lip, slimy water dripping onto the red clay bank.

"This one's a *big* daddy," he said. "Been caught before and got away—you can tell by the tear in his lip. See the way it's healed over?"

The crowd had grown while I was struggling with the rainbow. Six or seven men, now, were exclaiming over my catch, admiring its size and weight. I realized that they weren't praising me to make me feel good, the way adults often did. Each of them wished *he'd* caught that damn fish. Maybe it wasn't the Granddaddy Fish, but he was as impressive as he was ugly.

My father released the trout from the hook and stuffed its bulk into the creel, the mottled fan of its tail spreading out from under the woven lid, a reminder of its stubborn strength and glory. I'd done what he wanted, been a real boy, been victorious over that frantic bundle of muscle and instinct. He couldn't be disappointed in me now.

"Is that a good fish?" I asked, meaning: I didn't screw up, did I?

"Son, that's a *great* fish!"

"Then is it okay if I stop now?"

He gazed at me incredulously. "You want to *stop*? After catching the goddam king of the river?"

Staring desperately up at his lined, sunburned face, I wished I knew how to explain that my feelings were different than his.

"Dad," I said. "It's just more of the same. I get bored."

Recklessly, I met his gaze. He turned to the men still standing near us, a flash of anger deepening the color of the tanned crevices on his face.

"You hear *that*? You *hear* what my son said? He's bored! He caught the biggest damn rainbow any of us has seen all day and he's *bored*!"

"It wasn't *my* fault it bit on my hook. It might've taken *any*body's hook!"

"But *you* brought him in!" Then he looked at me and muttered, with a dismissing gesture of his big hand: "Go *on*—go back to the car and your reading."

The posture of his thick body told me more than words how disappointed he was, but I was nine years old and heartless. Without a backward glance, I walked upstream and across the road to where we'd left our car and the unresolved fate of the universe.

Three years later, after our ever-wandering family had ricocheted back to California, my father, still determined to make a sportsman of me, carried me off on a week's expedition into the Sierras, where, goddam it, I'd learn a man's appreciation of the outdoor life. Or else. He didn't realize that he was delaying the inevitable trajectory of his son's greatness. By then, I had no doubt that I'd be a great artist, writer, actor, politician—president, even. When greatness is in you, I'd read, you have to let it take you where it will and can't let anybody get in your way. Especially not your family.

Mom packed our food and we loaded fishing gear and camping equipment into our rocket-shaped, fin-tailed secondhand Dodge station wagon.

"Nothing like sleeping on a bed of pine boughs," dad told me. (A promise or a warning?) "And then waking up under the open sky. The trees and stars will be our tent."

I knew the reason we didn't have a tent was that we couldn't afford one, but actually I was looking forward to camping outside. However, I couldn't resist playing the character I'd built up for myself as a junior high school sophisticate.

"But," I protested, peering over the lumpy green sleeping bag writhing in my arms, "what if it rains?"

He frowned, then acting his own role of annoyed but tolerant father muttered, "we'll sleep in the back of the car. But it *won't* rain." Hands on my bony shoulders, he poured his cigarette breath into my face: "Understand? You're gonna have *fun*!"

My father loved to drive, and could—he often bragged—stay behind the wheel for days without stopping except to pee. So, to give us more time on the streams, he intended to drive straight through until we reached the mountains—even if it meant ten hours on the road.

"Don't overdo it," my mother cautioned him.

To her, he was all too often still a smart ass adolescent who couldn't resist showing off. It always delighted me when she spoke to him with the same tone of voice she used on me.

"Don't worry," he told her. "I never get tired driving. We're gonna have a great time!"

He looked at me with a fatherly smirk scarier than any horror movie.

I knew my dad tried to do his best for me, but to him I was simply "boy." Generic "kid." I was his son, but in his mind all boys were alike. He subscribed to *Boy's Life* for me because he had no doubt that I was like the boys in the stories it published. (And if I wasn't, it sure as hell wouldn't be his fault.) His own childhood had been shattered by divorce and frequent and disruptive relocations, so he gave me what he believed I needed as a boy, forcing our life together to fit the clichés about human nature he'd picked up from popular fiction and movies.

Damn it, he was doing the best he could!

Determined this time not to be bored, I strained to be fascinated by the gaudy billboards shooting past and the barns and cows and horses thrust like cardboard cutouts against the dirty brown hills. I gazed on California live oaks as if I'd never seen their twisted branches clawing at the sky and cross-examined my father about the rivers and forests we'd be exploring, but after a couple of hours my body started to be possessed. Without provocation, my twelve year-old arms and legs began to jerk and twitch. I changed positions, held my breath, and told myself a tale about intergalactic warfare, but nothing worked.

"Sit still," my father ordered, damp cigarette balanced on the edge of his lip, and launched into epic tales about when *he* went camping as a boy.

"In those days, fifty miles was an all-day trip. Roads were dirt and gravel, and you expected half-a-dozen flats, so you took along a tire patching kit. Every time you got a blow out, you stopped and took off the tire and dragged out the kit and fixed the inner tube and then put the tire back on. Took forever, but we had *good* times."

He said it like a challenge, his stubble-decorated chin thrust out, implying that *I* was too soft to know what a good time was, but the memories and their recitation improved his disposition. He almost forgot that I was there beside him as he stared at the two-lane concrete highway and saw himself jolting over the narrow dirt roads of the nineteen-twenties.

"Our old touring car didn't have a roof, so when it rained we got out and pulled up the canvas cover, snapping isinglass curtains on the sides. You couldn't see shit out of 'em, and they didn't keep out the weather, but they were what we had."

In the world of memory, everything happens in an eternal present. In memory, the boy who became my father still stands on a deeply rutted dirt road, watching his old man patch an inner tube so they can get the massive Hudson touring car rolling again. In memory, I still sit beside my dad as our bug-splattered Dodge station wagon struggles higher into the Sierras, maneuvering narrow, twisting roads used chiefly by loggers. The dusty car still pulls aside as logging trucks stacked with trees charge down mountain curves amid volcanic eruptions of red dust. My father still stops on a narrow WPA-era bridge above a rushing white and turquoise river, gripping my shoulder, hurting me in his excitement, as he says, "This is *it*, Petesy. The best goddamned trout fishing in California!"

Gazing at the turbulent water, I felt a perplexed awe; I couldn't deny that the redwood-edged torrent was both fierce and beautiful, but I couldn't imagine casting a fishing line into it.

As if reading my thoughts, he told me that we'd actually fish in hidden, quiet pools upstream, near where we'd be camping.

"You're gonna love it, Petesy," he commanded, and I felt overwhelmed with responsibility.

Leaving the two-lane paved road, we bumped over a logger's dirt track, the air around us choked with talcum-like vermilion dust. When the powder blinded us, dad got out and wiped off the windshield with a rag torn from an old plaid fishing shirt. On both sides of us, mottled, corrugated redwood bark rose higher than either of us could see from the car windows.

We drove under the cool shadows of ancient giants, as if moving through a dark hallway dusted by antiquity. Even I, unsentimental kid of the twentieth century, was impressed by this primitive world. My young eyes could spy a sail-backed dimetrodon cruising among broad ferns and a brontosaurus neck snaking around a thick coppery tree trunk.

And I did enjoy gathering redwood boughs for our beds and dry twigs for the fire, and then washing my hands and face in the frigid snow-fed river while dad heated our meal of beans and Spam. I even liked the way the food tasted, smoky and tangy and different than anything my mom ever cooked.

After rinsing the tin plates and utensils in the stream, my father got out the tackle. We had time for a couple of hours of fly fishing before dark.

"This is the best time—when the trout're feeding on the bugs skipping over the surface of the water."

And the bugs are feeding on us, I thought, swatting a mosquito.

Although certain I'd never enjoy fishing, I felt a reluctant excitement rising in me as we scrambled along the water's edge. The trees and river and all that nature stuff might be okay, but fishing had to be boring. Stubbornly, I dug my toes into the loose chocolate earth, following along with elaborate lack of enthusiasm. All this scenery had nothing to do with me. I hardly knew why I was there. I might as well have been in Oz or on Jupiter as in that prehistoric world high in the Sierras.

Trout fishing was the chief pleasure my father could drag from of a life of frustration and disappointment, but I didn't take time to think that out. I refused to give more of myself than I had to; only later did regrets begin to grow in the corners of my heart and mind.

Clattering birds teased us awake early the next morning and on the way to the river to fetch water to cook our oatmeal we surprised a hustling, hostile-eyed porcupine. Enormous, he swung his heavy, ruthlessly needled tail behind him in the red dust, like a medieval implement of war.

That day, dad and I experimented on the stream with new masterpieces from his hours at the kitchen table and waited for the "big one" to bite. We didn't talk much, but words weren't necessary in this man's world. Real men were silent, focused on their prey. Chattering and goofing off would scare the fish or deer or whatever we were pursuing.

The air under the high branches and among the dusty redwood trunks chilled us, but when we came to a clearing beside the stream, the sun reached down, warming our skin. My father drank from beer cans cooled in the icy stream, while I gulped at slippery bottles of 7-Up. The rocky bottom beneath the deceptively clear water seemed just inches from the surface, but my father told me that actually it was ten or twelve feet deep. Occasionally, irregular shadows skittered near the sheltered banks.

"Those are *trout*," he whispered, "the monsters we've come to get and take home."

The flickering sunlight on that mottled, rippling water made me dizzy. I was afraid I'd fall into the snow-fed river and be swept downstream until I crashed against a beaver dam or logging bridge, where I'd inhale the icy current and drown among broken, rotting logs. But when I tried to describe what I felt, dad told me to control my imagination and throw that fly out where the fish would find it.

"You've got too goddam much imagination," he scolded. "Facts're what you can count on: facts like busting your butt year after year to feed and clothe your family, facts like the time of day when the fishing is best and which are the right flies to use and how much a fat old rainbow weighs when you hold it in your hands. Facts, boy. *Facts*."

Shielding my eyes against the sunlight exploding from the streaked current, I looked at him: multiple suns burst like bombs from his round-framed glasses, but he aimed what was meant to be a reassuring smile at me, his cigarette-stained teeth several shades of yellow. And he and I pursued those damn rainbows, those German browns, trying to trick them into snatching the bits of feather and fur that disguised the barbed hooks at the ends of our lines. After all, who was smarter, who was craftier, those goddam fish or the two sports on the edge of the river bank?

Fear of the future struck my twelve-year-old chest like a redwood log, making me lose my balance so that I nearly toppled into the purple and green river, but I only sat down hard on the wet, sloping bank. The clear water rushed faster and faster over the rocks just beyond my mucky shoes, until my father grasped my collar and tugged me back to safety.

The fisherman's son forever, I could not escape my fate. In my dreams, I still must fish or die—until both my memories and my body are washed away at last on the currents of time. And the Granddaddy Fish is never caught, because he's always too damn clever.

15 Months

Geo. Staley

Once we get some good news at our check-ups,
most of us cancer folks are out the door
     and down the hall.
Not so this brain tumor boy and his mom
15 months into their cancer adventure.
They wait until
the dr. asks,
     Do you have any concerns?
In a practiced voice, the 9 yr. old answers
"Three."
He holds up a finger.
"One. When will my eye get straight?"
He catches his breath. Holds up a 2nd finger.
"Two. Will I be able to run and jump..."
There's tremor beneath the words.
     "...like everyone else?"
He looks at his fingers. Blinks.
"What was the question?"

We're Looking For a Cohesive Whole

Joan Payne Kincaid

In a labyrinth of nuns Zebras are running
across the screen
and why not? Words can't compete with them
even in a smart house
at 6:30 in the morning writing checks for charities
who have 4 hour lunches on my money;
it meant my morning music program was half over;

but I had to want to want to nearly scream
minding the blue cloudlessness.

Breakfast bacon was out on the dog- jump in the sun
defrosting for the eggs which really were only whites
in a bowl only the dog gets the yolk, get it?

Very life-like, and then we were finding the shady places
to include a 3-D transparency;
realizing summer is like every other season
mostly difficult to deal with especially because of the trees;
everyone keeps ignoring their need for water.

They left on vacation leaving a zoo of animals
to a place they never had come before;
it's comical the way the Zebras keep re-appearing
on screen and the nuns are riding them.
I'll never understand it but just like that they're galloping
across the veldt on screen
and you can't miss the new ribbon and spot light search box.

Dinner is watching some bozos wrestle an alligator
use the charts tab on the ribbon
but you decide to exit taking your linguini
with white clam sauce with you.

A Gecko for Breakfast,
or Christmas in Southern California

Suzanne Roberts

"Well there is one thing I might need help with," my mother admitted to my new boyfriend. "I'm having a small issue with a gecko."

It was the first time I was bringing my new boyfriend home to see my mother in Southern California. And it was not without trepidation. Since my father died, my mother has lived alone and manages to keep up with things around the house as best she can. But some things are harder to fix than others, and I knew it would make both my mother and my new boyfriend—who is very handy and practical—happy if he had a job to do while we were visiting. My mother tends to hover, so if I am checking my email, she rests her chin on my shoulder. And she has a rule that no one can be awake in the house if she is asleep, so she has to be the last one to bed and the first one up in the morning. It's either a serious case of Fear Of Missing Out, but more likely, a Fear Of Missing Out On Hovertime. Once I even caught her looking in through my window while I slept. "I was just watering the garden," she had said. But when I opened my eyes, I saw that look, the look I have seen on the faces of new mothers, peering at their brand new sleeping babies. But I'm 40 years old.

My boyfriend knew some of this, so if he could do a handyman job for her, one that she knew she wasn't qualified to supervise (though there are only a handful of such jobs), it could take pressure off us all. He would show off his Practical Boyfriend skills and my mother could concentrate her hovering on me.

I had not yet told my boyfriend my mother's philosophy on men, and though it isn't a theory I subscribe to, at least not wholly, I knew that my boyfriend's handyman skills would pave a way to her heart. "Men are good for three things," my mother had begun to say when my father died: "What they can do for you in the bedroom, what they can buy for you, and what they can fix for you." Then she would laugh but in that way that told me she wasn't joking, especially because she would continue: "If you want to have an interesting conversation, talk to a woman."

I would ask her, "What about a gay man?" to which she would concede that gay men are also good to talk to. And then I would ask "What about Daddy?" and my mother would be offended that I would dare to put my father into the category with Other Men. And for the record, my father never fixed anything that I know of, and he died broke. I'm not about to ask my mother about her third category for fear that she would, in fact, tell me all about it.

My mother, Practical Boyfriend, and I had just returned from spending Christmas Eve at Venice Beach, where the December sunshine glimmered off the breaking waves and the smell of salt air mingled with car exhaust. The difference between summer and winter in Southern California is the length of the day. Otherwise, with the surfers riding the waves, the children jumping into the spray, it could have been July. Practical Boyfriend is from the Midwest, so I thought he would enjoy a day at the beach as a novel way to celebrate Christmas. My mother and I were "raised Jewish," as Mother likes to say (Daddy was Jewish), so we've never had any set Christmas rituals.

We walked along the boardwalk, past the usual Venice char-acters—the electric guitarist on roller skates; the vendors selling sunglasses and t-shirts with pithy sayings like *I'M NOT A GYNE-COLOGIST, BUT I'M HAPPY TO HAVE A LOOK*; the fortune tellers burning sage; the Dead Heads still looking for a miracle; and the beefy men pumping iron at Muscle Beach. A group of four young men in neon t-shirts and flouncy pants were gathering a crowd with a megaphone—complete with siren—for their breakdance show.

"Let's stop and watch," I told my mother. "It'll be fun."

"Okay," my mother said, "Just watch your bag."

"It's fine," I said. "Don't worry."

She clutched her handbag and whispered into my ear, "They do this show so you won't pay attention when someone from the crowd—one of them—snatches your bag. It's all a distraction for the thieves."

"And the pickpockets?"

"Exactly. And don't you roll your eyes at me. I just saw a show on it." My mother clasped her purse in front of her with one hand and hung onto the shoulder strap of mine with the other. "You think I don't know about these things, but I do."

"Mom, please." I whispered. I didn't want Practical Boyfriend to hear her, though with the music and the megaphone, it was doubt-ful. I later learned he did hear her but did his best to ignore her pick-pocket paranoia.

"Just listen to me. You're too trusting. Remember that time those girls took your rings out of your locker in the seventh grade."

"I got them back."

"Well, you aren't always going to be that lucky."

As it turns out, I have left my purse in restaurants, theatres, and bars all over the world, and I have always gotten it back. Waiters and bartenders run after me, wondering if I left my backpack, my purse, my wallet, my glasses, my camera, my cell phone. I had always thought that perhaps my mother was right—I'm just careless. But now I realize that my carelessness is an act of defiance—even at 40. Our parents don't really want us to stop being their children, so sometimes, without meaning to, they make children of us, even when we are adults. And I've gone along with it, so my mother isn't wholly to blame. Or maybe it's just that we can't help becoming what we are expected to become.

We were able to outsmart the pickpockets and hold onto our purses, so we left the beach with all of our possessions. When we got back home, I asked my mother if she needed help with anything. If Practical Boyfriend could fix a leak or hammer a slat back into the fence.

That's when she told us about the small problem with the gecko.

"What do you mean you have a problem with a gecko?" I asked her. Practical Boyfriend, my mother, and I stood in the fluorescent lights of her kitchen.

"Well..." she said.

I was afraid to ask, but curiosity pushed me on. "What gecko?"

"It's here," she said. She moved over to the in-wall microwave oven and opened the door. It was stuck in the corner between the wall and the microwave, its claws reaching through the holes of the vent, its neck stretched and frozen, its eyes wide as if it was having a peek into the microwave, its tongue hanging from the desiccated mouth.

Practical Boyfriend just stood there, staring at his project. I have to say, it wasn't exactly what he was expecting.

"Mom, that's not a gecko. It's a lizard." Although my mother has lived in this country for more than 40 years, sometimes things that she wasn't used to growing up with in England—like lizards, kiwi fruit, avocado, and oleander—get called by the wrong names. Admittedly, there are three geckos indigenous to California, but they live in the desert and this creature stuck in my mother's microwave was not one of them. Crusty as it was, it was clearly a lizard.

"Well, I think he's stuck," my mother said and turned to Practical Boyfriend. "Do you think you can get him out?"

As you might imagine, Practical Boyfriend was speechless.

"Mom, how long has he been in there?"

"Oh, I don't know. About four months. Maybe five."

"So you haven't been able to use your microwave in five months?"

"Oh no. It works just fine. I open the door, say 'Hello gecko,' and then I put my bacon right there." She demonstrated her little wave to the lizard.

"Maybe we should get you a new microwave, Sheila," Practical Boyfriend said.

"Oh no. This one works just fine." My mother grew up poor in Northern England. Four of the kids shared a bed, even though the youngest was a frequent bed wetter. They used newspaper for toilet paper. They didn't own toothbrushes. There was no way my mother was going to get rid of a perfectly good microwave just because of a gecko.

"You've really been using the microwave this whole time?" I don't know why I asked because I very well knew the answer. And I now see that if this seemed at all odd to me, after growing up with my mother, how very strange it must have been for Practical Boyfriend. After meeting his family, I can say with certainty that not a one of them would ever cook her bacon alongside a dead lizard.

"Yes. It works fine," she said, as if the only issue here was the function of the microwave. My mother continued, as if she were trying to bring some normalcy to the situation: "And so the gecko wouldn't feel so alone," she went on, "I got him some friends." That's when I looked around and noticed the new décor: a gecko spoon holder, gecko dish towels, and two ceramic gecko wall ornaments.

"You decorated around the gecko?" I asked, even though the answer was obvious. Sometimes in my family, we repeat ourselves just to make sure we aren't in some surreal dream. When we realize we aren't, in fact, dreaming, we usually start laughing in that hysterical way that either makes us cry or pee. Practical Boyfriend just shook his head.

"Oh, I need the loo," my mother said and ran off to the bathroom.

"Can't we just get her a new microwave?" Practical Boyfriend asked.

"If you can't get it out, she'll just keep using this one. Because it still works. She'll be mad at us if we buy her a new one." I wiped away the laughter tears, hoping this would seem sort of, well, sort of normal.

"There's a dead lizard in it," he said as if this fact had just sunk in.

"Can't you get it out?"

When he said, "I can try," I was once again reminded what it means to be loved.

When my mother returned to the kitchen, Practical Boyfriend asked, "Where are your tools?"

"So you can get my gecko out? Oh, that'll be lovely. The tools are here," my mother walked toward the garage and Practical Boyfriend followed her. She showed him her wide assortment of tools—she works in a hardware store, a plan she originally hatched because she thought it would be a good place to meet a date. And it was, but to my mother's dismay, "All the do-it-yourselfers are cheap." But she is still there, selling garden hoses and barbeques. "I'm too young to retire," she claims. "All these people retiring in seventies and even in their sixties! It's ridiculous. Working keeps you strong."

Practical Boyfriend somehow managed to extract the dried-out husk of a reptile from the microwave, and in doing so, he scored major man points with my mother. Now the only geckos in Mother's kitchen are ceramic or the painted ones adorning dish towels. But when Mother offered Practical Boyfriend bacon on Christmas morning, he said, "I think I'll just have a banana."

The last time I spoke to her on the phone, my mother said, "You should see my rat."

"Is it alive or dead?" I asked.

"Oh, he's alive. He runs back and forth on my fence. *Shoom* one way and then *shoom* the other. What a tail he has!"

Knowing my mother as well as I do, I knew what to ask next: "You haven't been feeding him have you?"

"Well at first I thought he was a squirrel."

"So you *have* been feeding him? A rat."

"Maybe. But I think he might have been someone's pet. Like he escaped, and he's really meant to be a *house* rat." This is coming from a woman who recently asked me if I thought the mourning doves in her yard carried rabies.

"Like Snowflake and Snowball?" I asked.

When I was growing up, my mother and I kept pet rats, along with mice, hamsters, guinea pigs, rabbits, parakeets, fish, dogs, cats, and both a worm and ant farm. In our 700-square-foot apartment. My own mother's mother cooked her pet rabbit and drowned their kittens in the river, so in some ways I think my mother was trying to make up for it by turning our apartment into a mini-zoo.

"Exactly," my mother said. "Those were lovely rats, weren't they?"

I allowed that they were. At least Snowflake. Snowball was a bit of a biter.

Practical Boyfriend is now Practical Husband, and I haven't yet mentioned the matter of the rat to him. We're planning a trip to see my mother this holiday season, so why ruin a perfectly good surprise?

Third Generation

Kristin Bassett

Inheritance is an empty house
where wool dresses were lost

where they knit our pattern with foreign yarn
and set out plates
for those
whose hope displaced a thousand years
of us

while yours cast across the ocean
again and again

every half generation landing
at least a thousand miles from the last

and leaving each iteration alone.

That house is gone
but we are here

entwined
holding our own
on a string.

Contributors

Jeffrey C. Alfier is author of *The Wolf Yearling* (Silver Birch Press), *Idyll for a Vanishing River* (Glass Lyre Press) and *Terminal Island: Los Angeles Poems* (Night Ballet Press, forthcoming). His recent work appears or is forthcoming in *Spoon River Poetry Review*, *New York Quarterly*, and *Tulane Review*. He is the founder and co-editor of *San Pedro River Review*.

Chris Anderson is a Professor of English at Oregon State University and a Catholic deacon. He has written a number of books. His second book of poems, *The Next Thing Always Belongs*, was published by Airlie Press in 2011. He and his wife Barb have three grown children and live on the edge of McDonald Forest outside of Corvallis.

Kristin Bassett lives in Portland, OR. where she is a graduate student of literacy education at Portland State University.

Tobi Cogswell is a multiple Pushcart nominee and a Best of the Net nominee. Credits include or are forthcoming in various journals in the US, UK, Sweden, and Australia. In 2012 and 2013, she was short-listed for the Fermoy International Poetry Festival. In 2013, she received Honorable Mention for the Rachel Sherwood Poetry Prize. Her sixth and latest chapbook is *Lapses & Absences* (Blue Horse Press). She is the co-editor of *San Pedro River Review* (www.sprreview.com).

Thomas Elson was born, raised, and educated in the Plain States. A law school graduate with a degree in therapy, he worked in several states as a group therapist, then as a health center executive. He lives in Northern California.

Jeff Fearnside's poetry has appeared in *Permafrost, Qarrtsiluni, About Place Journal, Blue Earth Review, Assisi, Verseweavers, Protestpoems. org*, and *The Los Angeles Review.* He won 2nd Place in the Free Verse category of the Oregon Poetry Association Fall 2012 Poetry Contest (judged by Charles Goodrich), and his poems were twice named finalists in *Glimmer Train's* national Poetry Open contests. His chapbook *Lake, and Other Poems of Love in a Foreign Land,* winner of the Standing Rock Cultural Arts 2010 Open Poetry Chapbook Competition, was published in 2011 and additionally won the Peace Corps Writers 2012 Poetry Award. Other awards for his writing have included fellowships at the Bernheim Arboretum and Research Forest in Clermont, Kentucky; the Mary Anderson Center for the Arts in Mount St. Francis, Indiana; and the Andrews Experimental Forest in Oregon's Cascade Mountains. He lives with his wife and their two cats in Corvallis, Oregon.

Two chapbooks by **John Michael Flynn** appeared in November, 2013: *States And Items* from Leaf Garden Press (www.leafgardenpress.com) and *Additions To Our Essential Confusion* from Kattywompus Press (www.kattywompuspress.com). He also writes as Basil Rosa (www. basilrosa.com) and his novel *A Million Miles From Tehran* is due out in 2014 from Jaffa Books (www.jaffabooks.com).

Joan Frank (www.joanfrank.org) is the author of five books of fiction and a book of collected essays. Her last novel, *Make It Stay* (2012), won the Dana Portfolio Award; her last story collection, *In Envy Country* (2010), won the Richard Sullivan Prize in Fiction, the Gold *ForeWord Reviews* Book of the Year Award, and was named a finalist for the California Book Award. Her book of essays, *Because You Have To: A Writing Life* (2012), won the Silver *ForeWord Reviews* Book of the Year Award. A MacDowell Colony Fellow, winner of the Michigan Literary Award, Emrys Fiction Award, and Iowa Writing Award, three-time Pushcart Prize nominee and recipient of grants from the Ludwig Vogelstein Foundation, Sonoma Arts Council and Barbara Deming Fund, Joan is also a book critic for the *San Francisco Chronicle*. She lives in Northern California.

Sean Gill is a Brooklyn-based writer, playwright, and filmmaker who has studied with Werner Herzog and Juan Luis Buñuel, has followed public defenders for *National Geographic*, and was an artist-in-residence at the Bowery Poetry Club from 2011–2012. His written works have been published in *Full of Crow, Sein und Werden, Junta Juleil's Culture Shock, theNewerYork*, and *The Journal of Experimental Fiction*, among others.

Dianna Henning's work has appeared in, in part: *Crazyhorse, The Lullwater Review, Poetry International, Fugue, Swink, The Asheville Poetry Review, South Dakota Review, Hawai'i Pacific Review*, and *The Seattle Review*. Dianna holds a Master of Fine Arts in Writing from Vermont College of Fine Arts. Dianna taught creative writing for California Poets in the Schools, through the William James Association's Prison Arts Program and through California Arts Council grants. Her book, *The Broken Bone Tongue* (2009), was published by Black Buzzard Press, Austin, TX. Her first foray into fiction, a historical YA novel, *Seasoning the Blade*, was published in 2013 by Lucky Bat Books. Dianna has been twice nominated for a Pushcart Prize. She lives in Lassen County, California, with her husband Kam and malamute Sakari—here she finds inspiration in the vast stretches of land, the ponderosa trees, and abundant wild life. She facilitates The Thompson Peak Writers' Workshop.

Cindy Hines writes and lives in Portland, Oregon. She has worked as a freelance writer, journalist, grant writer, and technical writer. She graduated from Clackamas Community College with an AA in Elementary Education. She graduated magna cum laude from Lewis & Clark College with a BA in English, where she was the co-winner in the Academy of American Poets Prize competition. Her work has appeared in various journals and publications, including *Synesthesia*, *Synergia*, *The Lewis & Clark Literary Review*, *The Haraka Reader*, *Windfall*, and *Four and Twenty*.

Jayson Iwen lives in the Twin Ports. His poetry and prose have appeared in numerous journals, ranging from *Fence* and *New American Writing* to *Pleiades* and *Water~Stone Review*. He's won a number of literary awards and contests, including an Academy of American Poets Award, the Cleveland State University Poetry Center's Ruthanne Wiley Memorial Novella Contest, and the Emergency Press International Book Contest. His cross-genre novel *Gnarly Wounds* has just been published.

Christopher T. Keaveney teaches Japanese language and East Asian culture at Linfield College. His poetry has appeared in *Straylight Literary Magazine* and *Big River Poetry Review* and is forthcoming in

Syndic Literary Journal, Wilderness House Literary Review, Poetry Quarterly, and *Muddy River Poetry Review.*

Joan Payne Kincaid has been published internationally, and her new book is *Being Here: New and Selected Poems 1988–2012.*

Robert Kostuck is an M.Ed. graduate from Northern Arizona University. Recently published fiction and essays appear in *Clackamas Literary Review, The Massachusetts Review, Zone 3, The Southwest Review, Kenyon Review Online, Louisiana Literature, Tiferet, Alimentum, Fifth Wednesday Journal, Crab Creek Review, So To Speak, Flyway, Silk Road, EVENT,* and *Saint Ann's Review,* and are forthcoming in *Roanoke Review* and *Concho River Review.* He is currently working on short stories, essays, weavings, a novel, and the primary series of Astānga Yoga. His short story collection is seeking a publisher. He lives near an ocean; his heart belongs to the Chihuahua and Sonora deserts.

John P. Kristofco, from Highland Heights, Ohio, is professor of English and the former Dean of Wayne College in Orrville. His poetry, short stories, and essays have appeared in over a hundred different publications, including: *Folio, Rattle, The Bryant Literary Review, The Cimarron Review, Blueline, Poem, Avocet, Iodine, Small Pond, The Aurorean, Ibbetson Street,* and *Blue Unicorn.* He has published two collections of poetry, *A Box of Stones* and *Apparitions,* and has been nominated for the Pushcart Prize five times.

Richard Luftig is a past professor of educational psychology and special education at Miami University in Ohio who now resides in California. He is a recipient of the Cincinnati Post-Corbett Foundation

Award for Literature and a semifinalist for the Emily Dickinson Society Award. His poems have appeared in numerous literary journals in the United States and internationally in Japan, Canada, Australia, Europe, Thailand, Hong Kong, and India. One of his poems was nominated for the 2012 Pushcart Poetry Prize. He and his wife celebrated their 40th wedding anniversary.

Kathleen M. McCann has had poems published presses such as *The Threepenny Review, Midwest Quarterly, Big Muddy, Natural Bridge,* and *Witness.* Her second full-length collection of poems, *Barn Sour,* came out last year from Word Tech. Presently she is looking for a home for *Sail Away The Plenty,* a collection of poems about the Irish famine and its imprint on body, soul, and spirit. She is a die-hard New Englander and lives near the sea.

Bray McDonald is currently Senior Educator at the Tennessee Aquarium in Chattanooga, Tennessee. He lives in the historic community of St. Elmo at the foot of Lookout Mountain, where muses are numerous. Mr. McDonald has poems forthcoming in *Big Muddy, Stray Branch, The Cape Rock,* and *Iodine Poetry Journal.*

Kelly Miller has loved writing since she learned to scribble backwards on a Big Chief tablet and read the stories to her bears and dolls. Only recently has she begun sending pieces to literary magazines. When not writing, she works with autistic kids who always teach her more than she teaches them.

James B. Nicola has had 400 poems published in periodicals including *CLR, Atlanta Review, Tar River, Texas Review, Lyric,* and *Nimrod.*

A Yale grad and stage director by profession, his book *Playing the Audience* won a *Choice* Award. As a poet, he also won the Dana Literary Award, a People's Choice award (from *Storyteller*) and a *Willow Review* award; was nominated twice for a Pushcart Prize and once for a Rhysling Award; and was featured poet at *New Formalist*. His children's musical *Chimes: A Christmas Vaudeville* premiered in Fairbanks, Alaska—with Santa Claus in attendance opening night. His first full-length collection "Manhattan Plaza" is scheduled for 2014.

Scott Parker is the author of *Running After Prefontaine: A Memoir* and the editor of *Conversations with Ken Kesey*. "Cougar Dreams" is excerpted from his book in progress, *How Big the Bigness Is*.

Ricardo Pau-Llosa's seventh book of poems, *Man*, is from Carnegie Mellon UP. He is also a widely published art critic and a curator. Find more at www.pau-llosa.com.

Mike Pulley was a finalist for the 2013 *New Ohio Review* poetry contest. In 2008, he won a "Pioneer Poet" award in the Sacramento Metropolitan Arts Commission's Poets on Deck project. His work has appeared or is forthcoming in *Canary, California Quarterly, Tule Review, Poetry Now*, and *Cosumnes River Journal*. Pulley also is an award-winning journalist and teaches literature and advanced writing at Clemson University. He lives in Upstate South Carolina.

Bruce Douglas Reeves' novella, *Delphine*, published by Texas Review Press, won the Clay Reynolds Novella Competition. He also has published three novels (*The Night Action, Man on Fire*, and *Street Smarts*) and recently has completed a new novel and a pair of novellas. He has published short fiction in three dozen magazines and journals, both print and online, including *The High Plains Literary Review*, *Runner's World Annual*, *Hawaii Review*, *Eclipse*, *The Main Street Rag*, *Clapboard House*, *South Carolina Review*, *The Long Story*, *The Blue Lake Review*, *China Grove*, and *The New Renaissance*. He's married, with a daughter, Simone Martel, who also is a writer. He and his wife have visited more than sixty countries, some several times. His blog on Red Room has more information about him, his travels, and his writing: http://redroom.com/member/bruce-douglas-reeves/blog.

Charles Reneau loves to travel in wild mountains and deserts. His travels are both athletic and contemplative. He often returns home feeling emotionally renewed and physically sore. He carries a minimum of equipment, and tries to approach the land on its own terms. When the weather is cold, he is cold, too; when there is rain, he is wet. Through this process, he is trying to break down the illusion of separateness from his world and create photographs that express deep feelings of unity with the wild places in which he travels. Professionally, Reneau is a musician in the Oregon Symphony and faculty member at Portland State University. View more photos at reneauphoto.com.

Suzanne Roberts is the author of the memoir *Almost Somewhere: Twenty-Eight Days on the John Muir Trail* (Winner of the 2012 National Outdoor Book Award), as well as four collections of poetry. She writes and teaches in South Lake Tahoe, California. For more information, please visit her website: www.suzanneroberts.net.

Sandra Rokoff-Lizut, retired educator and children's book author (published by Macmillan, Holt Reinhart & Winston, and Hallmark

Inc.), is currently both a printmaker and poet. She is a member of Oregon Poetry Association, Mary's Peak Poets, Poetic License, Gertrude's, and a weekly writing salon. Rokoff-Lizut volunteers, by teaching poetry to middle schoolers, at the Boys and Girls Club in Corvallis, Oregon. She also studies poetry at Oregon State University. Along with her husband and three cats, Sandra lives in a simple-seventies house with a glorious garden.

Matt Schumacher, poetry editor of the journal *Phantom Drift*, has published two collections of poetry, *Spilling the Moon* and *The Fire Diaries*. New work is forthcoming in *Windfall* and *Western Humanities Review*.

Geo. Staley has retired from 25 years of teaching writing and literature at Portland Community College. He had also taught in New England, Appalachia, and on the Rosebud Sioux Indian Reservation. His poetry has appeared in *Chest, Four Quarters, Loonfeather, RE:AL Artes Liberales, New Mexico Humanities Review, Fireweed, Oregon East, Evening Street Review,* and many others. His non-fiction has appeared in such diverse publications as *The Journal of Thought, USA Today Magazine, Momentum, In-Ed,* and others. His first chapbook of poems, *Where Orphans Live,* was published in November 2003 by Finishing Line Press. His second, *Ready for Any Nuance,* was released February 2011, also by Finishing Line Press.

Christine Stewart-Nuñez is the author of five poetry collections: *Snow, Salt, Honey* (2012); *Keeping Them Alive* (2011); *Postcard on Parchment* (2008); *Unbound & Branded* (2006); and *The Love of Unreal Things* (2005). Her piece "An Archeology of Secrets" was a Notable

Essay in *Best American Essays 2012.* Her work has appeared in such magazines as *Arts & Letters*, *North American Review*, *Prairie Schooner*, and *Shenandoah.* She teaches creative writing at South Dakota State University.

Visit

clackamasliteraryreview.org
facebook.com/clackamasliteraryreview

Contact
clr@clackamas.edu

CLACKAMAS LITERARY REVIEW

the finest writing for the best readers

Clackamas Literary Review has been committed to bringing you the best writing from around the world since 1997. Subscribe now to receive the latest and forthcoming issues.

Clackamas Literary Review

_____	1 year	$10
_____	2 years	$18
_____	3 years	$26

Name _____

Address _____

City / State / Zip _____

Email _____

Send this form and check or money order to:

Clackamas Literary Review
English Department
Clackamas Community College
19600 Molalla Avenue
Oregon City, Oregon 97045

www.ingramcontent.com/pod-product-compliance
Lightning Source LLC
Chambersburg PA
CBHW071517170626
46811CB00007B/2880